JESSICA LAGRONE

BROKEN

BLESSED

GOD CHANGES THE WORLD
ONE PERSON
AND ONE FAMILY AT A TIME

Abingdon I
Nashvil

BROKEN & BLESSED
GOD CHANGES THE WORLD ONE PERSON
AND ONE FAMILY AT A TIME

Copyright © 2014 by Jessica LaGrone

All rights reserved.

Library of Congress Cataloging-in-Publication Data

ISBN 978-1-4267-7491-1

14 15 16 17 18 19 20 21 22 23—10 9 8 7 6 5 4 3 2 1
MANUFACTURED IN THE UNITED STATES OF AMERICA

TABLE OF CONTENTS

Introduction

IN MY FIRST SEMESTER OF COLLEGE, I signed up for a class called "Sociology of the Family." I slid into my seat on the first day of class just in time to hear our goateed professor open with a request: "Tell me about your family."

My heart started pounding as I looked around to see if I could excuse myself for a bathroom break and conveniently miss my turn, or maybe even hide unnoticed under my desk until the whole class exercise was over. There was nothi͗ I wanted to do less in that dingy, cinder-block classroor nan use my family history as some kind of introduction.

Having chosen a college that no one else from ᵢy hometown attended, I had claimed this year as m᷈ ꞇresh start: a chance to reinvent myself in a place wher no one knew anything about me. In my eighteen-year-oˡ mind, that precisely meant putting my most "normal" ꜚot forward in all circumstances. I wasn't completely sᵥ what normal was, but I knew what it was not: my fa ᵧy history of divorce, remarriage, redivorce, alcoholism, abuse, suicide, family secrets and family feuds, stepparents, step-cousins, step-grandparents, step-dogs, and step-cats. In my head it sounded more like a reading from the script of a soap opera than an explanation of my family tree. I was convinced this was not the first impression I wanted to make.

Then a surprising thing happened. The girl who went first said, "I didn't really grow up in a perfect family. My parents got divorced and remarried, but they only lived two streets apart, so we would spend one night at my mom's house and one night at my dad's. It was a weird way to grow up." The next guy said, "I don't really have a normal family either. My dad died when I was really young, and we moved in with my grandparents."

This pattern went on and on around the room. There was the guy who grew up visiting his dad in prison, and the girl who had been adopted from another country and looked nothing like her parents. There was the girl whose military family had moved around so much that she couldn't really say where she was from. There were people who had always felt different because they didn't have any brothers or sisters, and one person who felt like an anomaly because she had eight.

By the time most of the class had shared, *abnormal* was the new normal. And when my turn finally came, I was feeling much better about exposing my own strange family! What struck me as we went around the room revealing our family stories was that almost every person prefaced their introduction with a disclaimer that their family was "not perfect" or "not like everyone else's." Here I had been imagining that I was the only one whose family craziness made me crazy, when it turned out everyone else's family was perfectly imperfect too.

I expected families to fall into two categories. There were those like mine, the broken, and those with more perfect families, the blessed. I expected that classroom exercise to play out like a game of Duck, Duck, Goose, with turns going smoothly around the circle until someone (mostly me) would have to announce just how different they were. Instead, what I discovered was that each family was a mix, both broken and blessed.

I'm not sure where we first get the idea that everyone else's family is normal but ours. Many people, I'm afraid, get some of their ideas from church. On Sunday mornings everyone shows up in a matched set. A family. Each little unit walks into the sanctuary groomed and on their best behavior, clad in marital harmony and sibling adoration. No one would guess that almost every minivan that pulled into the church parking lot had, moments before, held tantrums and tension and mothers hissing through their teeth, "You'd better stop it this minute! We're at church!"

It so happens that the very book swinging at people's sides in their quilted Bible covers as they walk through the sanctuary doors holds story upon story of families who were troubled, messy, and chaotic. The family of the Bible looked nothing like the "perfect" family that my peers and I imagined. Starting at the very beginning of the Bible, in Genesis, was a family for whom sibling rivalry, parental favoritism, estrangement, and tension actually represented some of their better days. Incest, abandonment, and fratricide could be found on the pages of their worst.

If anyone had read some of the actual family stories from the first pages of our Bibles out loud in church, mothers would have covered their children's ears. Some families might have walked out in protest. Noah's son mocks his father's naked, drunken body. Abraham abandons his female slave and the son he fathered by her to die in the desert. Lot's daughters have sex with him out of fear that it's their only chance to conceive. How on earth did these stories make it into the Bible?

I imagine Joseph, the main figure in the final generation of Genesis family stories, sitting in my sociology class, forced to explain his family. Choosing his words carefully to edit out the worst parts, he might have started hesitantly like me. "You wouldn't know it from looking at us, but my family is strange. Our history is wilder than you could imagine," he says. "My family is not like everyone else's."

Except that they are. They are so different, so strange, that they are just like everyone else's strange and wonderful family. I can't help but picture God's exuberance over this first imperfect family that populated the earth, his joy in their misadventures and mistakes. "This is going to make everyone else feel a LOT better about their families!" he must have chuckled.

These were regular families with black sheep and stories

that made the neighbors talk. And these were the families that God chose. That he loved. That he used to impact the world in a big way. As we retell the stories of Genesis here, whispering the family gossip of centuries ago, we will see that if God can use these folks, we might be salvageable, too. There's something about finding God working through imperfect vessels that makes us want to offer our own on the altar. Once there, we find that God transforms us. Holy vessels often start out broken. The broken pieces of the Genesis family prove to us that God will heal and use and transform us, too, if we are available. We are ordinary, not perfect. But we can be used for extraordinary things. They certainly were.

I had been reading the book of Genesis for years, claiming it as one of my favorites, even before I realized it wasn't a loose assortment of individual stories, that the characters throughout the entire book are connected by one easily identified trait: they are all related. Their stories are collected into a family scrapbook and immortalized as the first volume in the best-selling book of all time. But whereas most families only paste the smiling, happy moments into their scrapbooks, the Genesis family scrapbook goes unedited. Here we flip past pictures of both their best and worst moments: the stories they chuckled over and retold again and again, and the ones they would be mortified that we're still telling today. These must be the most important stories to start with, since they are pasted here at the beginning. They must explain things we need to know about life and love and family. If we pay attention, they may even make their way into our own scrapbooks, transforming the way we see our own stories of learning and growing and living: imperfect people have a place right up front in God's story.

When I began to read Genesis as a family story, it helped me understand that God wasn't waiting for me to get my act together to start loving me. If God chose this peculiar family to change the world, then maybe he could do something with my less-than-picture-perfect family, too.

My hope in retelling the Genesis family stories here is to help us pay attention to the beauty of the broken moments, to learn to thank God for including the trash alongside the treasure so that we can recognize that we're not alone, not abnormal after all.

Despite our best efforts, families often end up full of flaws and fights and not-so-photo-worthy moments, but it turns out that's not a glitch in the system. Families are imperfect because of the material from which they are made: people. We walk around flawed and broken all the time, but we're great at hiding the cracks. Among family, our weaknesses are no secret from one another. We let our guards down. It's the place where we are fully known, hoping that we will be fully loved. Together we can read and discover something about a family from another time, and find our own stories transformed and shaped for new purpose. The stories we are hesitant to tell may be the ones that have the most purpose after all.

"Tell me about your family."

That first day of sociology class crumbled the idea that everyone else's family was normal but mine. Maybe the goal wasn't to fit your family into some mold called perfect or at least throw a blanket over it all and pretend with all your might that there was no mess underneath. Maybe our families were the cracked ground we had all sprung up from, gritty and holey and good for growth. We were, all of us around the circle that semester, standing on the cusp between the families we came from and those we were headed for, the faults and gifts of the past becoming clear just as our dreams for the future began to take shape. We were so much wiser than those who raised us. Now we're treading the same water. What in the world will my kids say on that first day of class when they are asked, "Tell me about your family"? As they sink down low in their seats, I hope they look back with a forgiving eye.

Genesis is a story thick with beauty not because the people found there are particularly strong or exceptionally good. They are simply a family that accepts God's embrace. In their stories we find that the unit in life that sometimes causes the most pain and alienation is also the place we are likely to receive the most joy. It's possible to be both broken and blessed.

This is a book about reclaiming the stories that shaped us, reclaiming our own family stories—both the stories of our immediate family and the stories of our much more ancient family, the family of the people of God. In this book, history will knock at our door: the ancient history of biblical families and, if we let it, our own family histories. I am inviting you to remember the broken spots of your own family tales, and hold them up next to the broken places in the family of God, and I am inviting you to remember that you are blessed. Since the beginning of time, God has been creating blessing from our broken family histories. This is a book about each one of us taking our place at the family table.

CHAPTER 1

In Search of Beginnings
Chaos

BURIED WITHIN ALL OF US is a longing to know where we come from, what kind of stuff we're made of. It's why researching genealogy has become such a booming hobby. Why children love to hear the story of the day they were born. Why everyone still listens when grandpa spins the same old family tales again and again.

Where did I come from? Far more than a reproductive question, this question strikes at the heart of who we are. Many of us dance around it for decades. For my friend Tara, it was a way of life.

Tara recognized she was different from an early age because she was adopted. Even though she felt loved and accepted by her family, she always felt a sense of longing that she couldn't explain—a longing to know where she came from. To know her roots, her heritage.

When people would talk about their family coming over on a boat to Ellis Island, or an ancestor who fought in the Civil

War, she would get a pang of loneliness for her own history. The longings would happen at the strangest times. She once waited tables in a restaurant for two men having lunch, and noticed that the sound of their laughter was identical—it was obvious that they were father and son. Another time she was looking at some pictures of a friend and her mother, who at first glance didn't look that much alike. But when she looked closer she saw that her friend's hands looked just like her mother's, a tiny piece of heredity tucked away in the details.

Tara wondered, *Who does my laugh sound like? Whose hands look like my hands?* All of this longing to know her origins was wrapped up with the fact that her adoptive father died when she was seven, and she had vivid dreams about the man who was her birth father. What did he look like? Did he think about her? Was she missed?

Finally, Tara decided to stop wondering and do something about it. So she went to the courthouse in the county where she was born and asked to see her original birth certificate, but the records were sealed. She learned, though, that somehow the system had overlooked one little clue.

The state had transferred the same identification number from original birth certificates to adoptive birth certificates. While the birth certificate she had did not have her birth parents' names, it did have a number: 560603. If she traced that number back through the records, she might be able to locate her birth mother's name. She held her breath, wondering if this could be the piece that would unlock the history she had longed for.

In the basement of the courthouse, Tara discovered that the records from the 1960s weren't computerized. They were kept in huge, dusty books. She sat in a dimly lit room with the first yellowed book in front of her and followed her finger down the margin, fifty-six entries per page, seventy thousand births in the year she was born.

Since the records were arranged alphabetically by the mother's last name, a name she didn't have, she would have to manually look through all the lines of records, scanning the six-digit numbers for one that matched her own: 560603. After a few hours, her eyes began to play tricks on her. Her vision swam and then snapped back to attention. Once in a while she would come across a number that was just one digit off. For just one second, her heart would jump in her chest, like hearing you got one or two of the numbers on the winning lottery ticket. But then she would realize it wasn't a match, and that she had to keep looking. She left when the courthouse closed its doors and returned the next day. She came back every day for five weeks.

Finally, one day when she was almost at the end of the alphabet, her finger landed on a number. She matched the digits one by one: 560603. She checked it again. And again. Next to it she found her birth date and an *F* for female.

At the beginning of that line was a last name. And then a first: Suzanne. Tears welled up in her eyes as she said over and over again to herself: my mother's name is Suzanne.

When she went to make a copy of the page, her hands were shaking so much she couldn't work the machine. The clerk looked at her a little strangely as she helped her push the button.

All Tara could say was, "I found my mother. My mother's name is Suzanne."

Many of us yearn to know more about the tribe we came from. Some of us can sketch our story back through a few generations. Others know the events and names that began forming us centuries ago. The truth is that if we search far enough back, climbing limbs up the family tree, we all eventually find the same origins. The same story. The one that starts with these words: "In the beginning."

That's what our hearts long for, to know our beginnings.

The Bible (our "Genesis"), that ancient, dusty book, starts giving up answers not on the last page, but on the first. "In the beginning God created the heavens and the earth." (Genesis 1:1 NIV)

This is our story. The story of where we come from. If we trace our fingers over that first sentence, our hearts might leap as if the numbers all lined up for the first time.

This is where our story starts. This is where our family begins.

Genesis. The word literally means "beginning." If you open a Latin translation of the Bible, the first word you read is "Genesis"—a single word we've stretched out to the phrase "In the beginning."

Genesis is a book of beginnings. It is deeply concerned with the origins of things—of the universe, of humankind, of relationships, of sin, of civilization, of families, and of one special family created and chosen by God to be the instrument through which he would bless the world. That family is our family, yours and mine. Like all good family stories, it starts not just with a something or somewhere, but with a someone.

In the beginning God.

My background is in biology, an area that intrigued me because I have always felt close to God when admiring the intricate details of his creation. Genesis begins with the story of how everything we know came to be, but it's always seemed a little short on details for me. When I read the creation story, the biologist in me wants to know *how*. How did all this happen? How does it fit with the fossil record, evolutionary theory, the existence of other planets? How long did it all really take to unfold?

But when I search this story for the details of *how*, what I discover instead is that this story is all about the *who*.

And while all of the things we see and experience in this world have their beginnings in Genesis, this *who* is the one exception. In a story of origins, we are introduced to a God who has no beginning and no end. When we open the first page, he's already there. When we close the last page, he is to be continued. He is the one exception to the rule: everything else we know has to be created from the ground up. From scratch.

I've found there are really two kinds of families where

beginnings are concerned: those who believe in creating from scratch, and those who don't. Some people just love to spend hours in the kitchen surrounded by counters piled high with canisters of flour and tiny boxes of *herbs de provence* (whatever those are.) I'm much more comfortable handling a box of Hamburger Helper.

I came from a family where our philosophy in the kitchen was, "If God made a mix for that, it was his way of telling me I shouldn't have to make it from scratch. Praise God from whom all Betty Crocker flows." My husband, Jim, on the other hand, came from a family that instilled in him the motto, "If you can make it from scratch, why would you use a mix?" For them it's some kind of badge of honor to say that no boxes were harmed in the making of a meal.

The months following our wedding confirmed the truth that every marriage is cross-cultural. It doesn't matter if you both come from the same ethnic background, the same side of the tracks, even from the same side of the street. It's only when you end up in the same household that you realize the vast chasm of how you were raised: the way you load the dishwasher, the correct method to fold a towel, the type of peanut butter you buy. It's not the big stuff—philosophies of childrearing, religious affiliation, how you manage finances—that always plagues marriages. The decisions that force friction sneak up on you in tiny ways. Crunchy or creamy?

So when we got married, we had some work to do. When it came to the cooking debate, we did what every successful couple eventually does: we compromised. If he wanted something made from scratch, he could make it himself. And the great thing was that he did! It has actually been an arrangement that both of us enjoy. He enjoys making things, and I get to enjoy eating them: homemade ice cream, homemade bread, homemade granola. (I didn't even know it was possible to make granola from scratch!)

One of the reasons I don't try to make things from scratch (or at least one of my favorite excuses) is that I know the truth. There's no such thing.

There is no creating from scratch. Carl Sagan said, "If you want to make an apple pie from scratch...you must first create the universe."

You and I can't create from scratch because we can never really make anything out of nothing. All of our supposed ingredients are actually the results of a recipe God finished long ago. This is an astounding fact if you think about it for long.

"In the beginning God created the heavens and the earth. Now the earth was formless and empty, darkness was over the surface of the deep" (Genesis 1:1-2 NIV).

In the beginning the earth was not much to look at. It was like a bowl of raw ingredients. Not the brownie batter (from a mix if you're making it with me) that tempts you to taste, but the dense, tacky, bowl of prebaked meatloaf matter. Odds are it will turn out great eventually, but no one wants to eat a spoonful just yet. Creation was still a little half-baked.

Here's something about God: he must love a challenge, because this recipe starts out a mess. It's chaotic and empty and dark. And it clearly isn't going to just whip itself into shape. That's his job. It's into this chaotic, empty, dark place that God begins to speak. "And God said, 'Let there be light,' and there was light" (Genesis 1:3 NIV).

The first thing God tackles in creation is darkness. It's an important starting point. It gives us a glimpse into just how much God and darkness are at odds with one another. "This is the message that we have heard from him and announce to you: 'God is light and there is no darkness in him at all.'" (1 John 1:5)

God will not let darkness rule the earth. Those first words set into motion a pattern of behavior that will become predictable because God hates darkness. Where there is darkness in our lives, our families, our world, we can be assured that God is speaking light into corners dark with trouble and despair. This is one reason that family secrets never work.

"Your uncle is a drug dealer and he lives in a jail." Haley was eight years old when she heard those words ring out from a little girl on the merry-go-round across the playground. Haley and her siblings had been told their uncle was in the military, overseas on extended duty, but the minute she heard the words, something told her they were true. When her parents asked her later why she punched the girl in the mouth, she told them it was because she didn't want her little brother to hear. She was already learning to conceal from him what her parents had hidden from her.

Hiding something under the cover of darkness doesn't reduce its potency; it only causes it to spoil, to begin to stink like the leftovers in the back of the fridge—the green fuzz feeding on what has already gone bad. God is in the business of bringing things into the light. Phototherapy.

In the act of lighting darkness in creation, God is just getting warmed up. If creation soup starts out formless, empty, and dark, God sets up shop by bringing the opposite into being.

- God forms order out of chaos.
- He fills emptiness.
- He lights darkness.

Every good résumé is packed with verbs: *forming, filling, lighting*. This is a job description that will last far beyond just an itinerary for the first few days of earth.

Knowing that God could have chosen to get things started in any way he wanted to, we might ask why page 1 doesn't open right away onto a picture of glowing beauty, order, and light. I think God wanted to show us what he can do with raw material, a little nod to those of us who are still feel slightly half-baked: those with struggling families, cracked relationships, lives that can't quite seem to get it together, and a world that's showing a little wear around the seams. When God wants to create the remarkable, he chooses to work with the less than perfect. As Genesis unfolds, we will be grateful for that simple fact, since the family he chose and blessed was perfectly imperfect—and every family since has been as well.

God's partiality for order shows up almost as quickly as his distaste for darkness. The clues pointing to beauty and order even shape the words and language of the first chapter of the Bible. It is poetic and lyrical, but with the precision of a military cadence: Evening and morning, day one. Evening and morning, day two. Evening and morning…and it was good, it was good, it was very good.

God begins shifting, separating, clearing the way for the majesty that is to come, separating light and darkness, earth and sky, land and water. The way he clears space for the incredible fullness of the world as we know it reminds me of cleaning house: separating lights and darks, junk mail and bills, piles of what belongs in this room and that. Everything has a place and everything in its place.

The metaphor for homemaking is a fitting one here, since God is literally making a home for every being that will ever live throughout the successive eras of history.

In first-century Judaism, it was the husbands who were the homemakers. When the families of a bride and groom settled on an engagement, the proposal was a binding agreement, more of a contract than a romantic photo op. They took betrothal so seriously that canceling a wedding was the equivalent of divorce.

One of the major differences between their culture and ours is that our engagements are often spent preparing for the wedding—hard work that, let's face it, falls mostly on the bride. For the first-century Jewish couple, however, the hard work during the engagement was for the groom. With such a binding betrothal in place, the only things that stood between the couple and marriage were a ceremony and a house.

Immediately after the proposal, the groom would begin building a home for his future wife and family on his family compound. Only when it was completed could he return to his bride to tell her that their home was ready and the wedding ceremony could begin.

First the home. Then the family.

That's an unusual practice for us to wrap our minds around. But in this earlier society, the home came first. That's the order that Genesis takes: first a home, then a family. It's only toward the end of chapter 1, when the environment is complete, that the human inhabitants are given the keys and invited to move in.

With the lights already on, the rest of God's job description of forming order from chaos and filling the emptiness are in full swing. He spends the first three days of creation forming environments, and the next three days filling them with inhabitants.

The pattern is unmistakable.

- The environment created on day one (light and dark) is filled with the inhabitants of sun, moon, and stars on day four.
- The environmments created on day two (sky and sea) are filled with the inhabitants of fish and fowl on day five.
- The environment created on day three (dry land) is filled on day six with the inhabitants of animals and, finally, human beings.

First a home. Then a family.

Each of these sets of inhabitants will have a special relationship with the environment they were created to fill, fitting hand in glove. And no being will have such a unique or more connected relationship with its environment as the human family.

I can imagine that first-century groom working with such care on the house he was building for his bride. With every nail, every board he put into that home he must have thought of her. He thought of her living there, enjoying the home he had made. He thought of the life they would have there, the children they would raise there together. The day he completed the house would have to be the day he had been looking forward to all along because it meant he finally got to be with her.

As he began his journey back to the bride's family to share the news that their home was complete and the ceremony could commence, the first tradition of the wedding celebration began. Friends who noticed where he was going and the new excitement in his step would run ahead, beating him to the bride's house to announce the good news that her wedding day had arrived. All along the way they would shout out a phrase to everyone in their path. They would shout it in the streets until they reached her house, and then they would shout it up to her window: "The bridegroom is coming! The bridegroom is coming!"

When God builds the house, the goal isn't just structural integrity (although imagine anything man-made standing up to the wear and tear the earth has been through) or aesthetic beauty (which it has in spades). The goal is to prepare a place for a relationship to happen, for bridegroom and bride to live alongside each other, for God and his people to grow closer in intimacy and affection. This whole creation is the stage for a very special relationship, one between homebuilder and home dwellers, to be born, to be nurtured, to thrive.

Relationship. That's the point. The real purpose we're created for.

That was what drove Tara's longing to know her past, what fueled the hours in the courthouse basement: not just the start to her story, but a connection to the people who were there when it all began. A relationship. The name she discovered wasn't the end of her search. It was just the beginning.

Tara's search into her murky past uncovered a name that she held in trembling hands: Suzanne. Using the information she had copied from the book and the modern magic of Google, she discovered a Suzanne of about the right age who still lived near the city where she had been born.

Tara spent days trying to compose a letter. Just how does one say the words, "I think I am your daughter"? After several drafts, she handwrote the letter on carefully chosen paper, said a prayer, and stuck it in the mail. In reply she got a hesitant letter, filled with questions. Guarded. It asked, "What makes you think I'm the woman you're looking for?" Tara sent a photocopy of the page from the big dusty courthouse book. She also sent an essay she had written about being adopted and searching for her family.

The e-mail she got in reply said, "You're a wonderful writer. Your father was a wonderful writer, too." Tara's breath caught in her throat at that phrase. "Your father…" The e-mails began to warm up a bit, become more curious and friendly. She sent Tara a birthday card a few weeks later, marking the only day that they had ever laid eyes on each other decades before. As Tara put it later: it was a huge, huge, huge deal to get that card.

They began by taking it slow. Cards and e-mails and an awkward but happy phone call were all that marked the beginning of the gradually unfolding relationship. Suzanne was happy to fill in some blanks for Tara as they got to know each other but wasn't ready quite yet for face-to-face contact. This was a huge deal for her, too, one she didn't believe would ever happen. That's been hard for Tara, but she's trying to be understanding and patient until Suzanne is ready.

Suzanne did, however, pass along information about Tara's birth father. Again, Tara sat down to compose a special letter, and after it arrived she immediately received an e-mail in reply, this one from her birth father, the man whose face she had dreamed about since she was a child. The first two sentences made her heart skip a beat:

"This is epic. I've been waiting almost forty years for this letter." He signed the first e-mail, "Love, Frank."

A few e-mails later he began signing, "Love, Dad."

He sent her a picture of him, from years earlier, a young girl who was Tara's half sister giggling in his lap. Tara stared at the picture for a long time, going over every little pixel. She noticed his hand resting on the girl's shoulder, and there was an instant recognition: "His hand looked exactly like mine. I have his hands. I can't tell you what that was like. Finally there was a piece of me in someone else. Those are my hands."

When Frank learned Tara was saving up for airfare so she and her kids could fly across the country to meet him, he bought the tickets himself and sent them to her. When I last talked to her, she was giddy and nervous, anticipating the moment when she would step off a plane and look into her father's eyes for the first time.

This is raw material, dark and chaotic: our family stories, the deep corners where our creation happens. In the best of circumstances, families are the instruments through which God forms, fills, and lights our existence. In the worst, we find in them chaos, emptiness, and darkness. If we are honest, all of our families are muddy, earthy things, jars of clay into which are poured some of the worst and best scenes of our lives. There is nothing more intimate, nothing more personal, nothing that pushes our buttons for both good and bad further than our families. Whereas for many the family is a place of light and warmth, for others, family is a place where darkness overshadows hope. The good news is that wherever there is chaos, wherever there is emptiness, wherever there is darkness, there is God, hovering over the waters, poised to act, speaking light and love and the beginning of something beautiful.

Where do I come from? The answers to that question can be comforting, perplexing, and heartbreaking. No matter what chaos we find in our murky beginnings, we will find God there as well. None of our stories are untouched by the madness and mess of humanity's origins. Some are messier than others. But the sweet payoff of uncovering those origins is that we find God there too. If we find him in the mess of our yesterday, then he will be more easily found in our today and our tomorrow as well.

Tara went in search of her Genesis. What she found there wasn't all sweetness and light. Uncovering what has been hidden is always a doubtful reach into the back of the refrigerator—the ingredients for scratch alongside the Tupperware filled with things hidden from the light for far too long. But somewhere in that murky past, Tara had a loving father, shrouded in mystery, waiting to be discovered. Going after our Genesis is worth it.

This is our past. Our family story. This is epic.

CHAPTER 2

Lost in the Garden: Adam and Eve
Creation

WHEN GOD CREATED THE WORLD, he chose to start it all with a family. He easily could've opened the curtains on creation to reveal a community or even a city teaming with people from the very beginning. He could've made the first collection of people neighbors or coworkers, but he chose to start with a family: a man and a woman positioned side by side in a garden to parse the ins and outs of the fledgling world together. The primary unit for human existence is the family.

The world started with a family, and it is within family that we all have our start. When all is as it should be, it is here that we discover what it's like to be treasured, protected, watched over. Those early and semiconscious revelations give us the clues we need to discover, when we are ready, that we are the center of God's heart. God's love is such a big thing that it takes practice being created by someone, belonging to someone, being chased after and nursed by an earthly someone, before we can even fathom Divine Love.

I grew up alternating back and forth on holidays between my mom's household and my dad's, since they divorced very early in my life. My dad's extended family gathered en masse once a year, at Thanksgiving. They were a very male-centered clan, with four brothers and their wives, their father and their mother (my grandmother) a flurry of domestic activity who orbited around the needs and preferences of each of her boys. I marveled at how she remembered and cooked each of their favorite foods and desserts, no matter how large the family grew. Each Thanksgiving, I landed in this plot that was both alien and familiar. So much about me was very different from this extended family, and yet in them I recognized where different pieces of me had their origins. Back at my mom's, I was considered strange for my tendency to oversalt my food, my night owlish ways, and what were deemed antisocial behaviors. Here I had to fight for the salt shaker at the dinner table. Here the tendency to stay up past midnight and sleep in was accepted without question. Here I could stand side by side with my granddad in silence, staring at the ground outside in the yard, and realize we had communicated more with two sentences passed between us in half an hour than most people did with volumes of conversation. I hadn't seen many of these people in a year. They were strangers to me in some ways, but I also felt a deep sense of belonging. The DNA within me seemed to sing out in such close proximity to its origins. The fact that I was ordinary among them somehow made me feel special.

Family is a place where we are exceptional despite the fact that everyone knows how ordinary we actually are. No matter if you're a big shot in the workplace, on the sports field, or even in the media, they are those people who just shake their heads and say, "I knew him when." Whatever our bragging rights in other circles, when we return to our families they know immediately if we're just bragging.

This is at once comforting and maddening. To have your hair tousled by great-aunt Margaret on holidays—whereas back at work they call you sir or doctor or even Your Honor—can be annoying, but it can also bring a relief that someone in the world sees past your facade of importance. No matter who you are or what newspaper your picture is on the cover of, somewhere there is someone who knows that you were afraid of the dark until you were eleven, that you struggled with long division, that you cried when your best friend moved away.

Family may be the clearest image of the love of God that we can ever have, because they love us before we ever do anything to deserve it. No one gazes down at their newborn and says, "All right kid, the jury is still out on you. I'll get back to you in a few years on whether I love you or not. We'll have to see how you turn out." Instead, we lavish deep affection on those who have done nothing to win us over except belonging to us. We are the ordinary treasures of the people we love.

Believing that God could love us at face value, without any deserving act on our part, takes practice. We are assigned a group of people at our point of entry on earth primarily for that task, to love us because they have to, and because they get to.

23

When we learn, sometime later, that in God's vast office of the universe, ours is the picture he places at the center of his desk and gazes at, we can't help but automatically deny the possibility it could be true. In a world that contains the Alps and supernovas, chameleons and sequoias, it's a stretch to think that God is most proud of, most interested in our meager existence. It takes the love of visible humans to teach us that lesson over and over again before we can accept it from an invisible God.

The human family is the pinnacle of creation, the heart of God's workplace, even though we come from humble beginnings. Just in case we get too puffed up with the idea that we are the best of God's handiwork, there's always the knowledge that we are made from common, run-of-the-mill dirt, the kind we shake off our boots and sweep from our floors. God simply scooped up some ground and shaped the first human, no more exclusive than a child's mud pie.

"Then the LORD God formed a man from the dust of the ground and breathed into his nostrils the breath of life, and the man became a living being" (Genesis 2:7 NIV).

There's something very grounding in the memory of digging into the clay in my backyard as a five-year-old, trying to find enough raw material to create a simple cup or bowl. The dream that something of my creation could be useful, could even be placed on our breakfast table and filled with food or drink, was for some reason thrilling to me. Children often play at work—measuring their actions by usefulness in the real grown-up world, while adults work hard at play, doing their best to return to the ease of childhood.

There's a kind of wordplay going on here in Genesis between the ground (the Hebrew *adamah*,) and the word for *human*—not the male word *man* but *human*, the word that encompasses both male and female, *adam*. That's where the first person gets his name, Adam. Human.

That undeniable similarity between *adamah* and *adam* reveals a rootedness that goes beyond etymology. Of all the spaces that God has filled with inhabitants, he gives humans an unmistakable connection with their environment, the earth. Humans have the ability to make sure that when they flourish, their environment benefits. When humans sin, their environment suffers along with them.

Dirt is not the only ingredient that goes into what it means to make a human. Into this dusty creature, as common as the ground we walk on, God breathes the breath of life. Suddenly we are not simply ordinary. We are infused with God's own breath, the same breath that hovered over the waters in Genesis 1. We learn something very special about ourselves in this passage—about the balance of our ordinariness and the extraordinariness of God that fills us with life. In an already incredible world, there is something exceptional about us.

Humans aren't just the inhabitants, filling the environment of earth. We're also an environment created for the One Holy Inhabitant to occupy, filling us with his image, his breath.

"Or don't you know that your body is a temple of the Holy Spirit who is in you? Don't you know that you have the Holy Spirit from God, and you don't belong to yourselves?" (1 Corinthians 6:19).

What are we? We are dirt-cheap containers filled with the most precious stuff possible. Of all the holy places on earth that God could have chosen to reside, he chose to make us his temple. The human family will forever be faced with the choice to treat each other like dirt, or to recognize in one another the image of God.

What intrigues me most about this first garden is how the Gardener made it such fertile soil for perfect relationships to grow. We still interact in these same connections, but their perfection there in the beginning was so pure that it is now hard for us to even picture.

- Man and woman, who were made for each other, lived in loving harmony.
- Humans tended their environment, and in return it supported them with food and life and beauty.
- And possibly most remarkable of all, there is the description of the intimate relationship between the people and their Creator God.

Genesis quite simply and beautifully pictures them walking together in the garden in the cool of the day. No big deal—just a regular stroll with the most powerful being in the universe. That has always made me slightly envious of the intimate chance they had to know and converse with their Creator.

What must it have been like to walk so closely with God that you could stand right next to him—with no sin standing between you, no guilt, no past, no feelings of inadequacy or regret? The very best gift in all of Eden was how God gave us himself, no strings attached.

God handed them the world on a platter: all the beauty they could take in, all the food they could eat (with one small exception), a marriage made in heaven between two people who could say they were made for each other, no pain, no sickness, no death, no taxes, no rush-hour traffic or terrible twos.

We have no real idea of how long things went on this way, in the perfect world before creation cracked. Maybe the constricting force of time itself only broke in once the world hit its downward spiral. What we do know is that the odds of millions of right choices against the one wrong choice were not enough to hold back the force of human curiosity. Children left alone and allowed to watch television "except that one channel" know how the remote beckons. The forbidden food that is off our diet cries out to us from the back of the refrigerator. The one bad habit, the one toxic relationship, whatever the voice that we know we should not follow, we all know how loud its insidious whisper can be. The humans on Perfection Street must have heard its call on repeated days, maybe even years, before they gave in. But give in they did, with hands that picked and mouths that ate, and a whole world that felt the devastating effects.

That first sin spun into motion a series of reactions that have traditionally been called The Fall. When something is epic enough to have a capital The in front of it, it usually brings with it an impact widely felt and a shared history that follows. When communities refer to The Storm or families refer to The Accident or The Diagnosis, we know their lives still sting from the effects of their The event.

To me, *Fall* always seemed like a poor choice of words, because a fall sounds like something that happens by accident. You're walking along. You slip. You don't mean to. You fall down. Oops. Somehow that just doesn't fit here.

My three-year-old son has an extensive vocabulary, something that his teachers and even those who meet him in the grocery store comment about. But somehow he is having difficulty grasping the difference between the concepts of *accidentally* and *on purpose*. My marker *accidently* wrote on the wall. Did you hit your sister? Yes, *accidentally*. In truth, there was a lot of purpose in those actions.

Even the baby in our family, at a year old and with a much more limited vocabulary than her brother, is having trouble with the concept of accidental versus on purpose. One of her favorite games is to sit in her high chair and to take all that lovely and nutritious food we've placed in front of her (did I mention her father makes baby food from scratch?) and throw it violently on the floor. And then look innocently up at me with her wide blue eyes and say, "Uh oh!"

The first sin, the one we've christened The Fall, isn't really an "Uh oh" sort of event. It's far from accidental. Sin rarely is. There was no "Oops, how did that fruit get in my hand?" No uh-oh. If you ask me it was less of a Fall and more of a Jump, a Leap away from God. The results were disastrous on all levels. The relationships God had intended as gifts broke wide open and revealed human shame, inadequacy, blame, and fear. The primary broken relationship is between God and humans, and all other relationships will suffer as a result.

The perfect world is perfect no more. Now we will feel the ache of distance from God in shame and guilt, that feeling of our prayers hitting the ceiling and bouncing back down on us. Now our relationships will involve feuds and spats and resentment and passive-aggressive cold shoulders, Eve expecting Adam to read her mind and Adam trying to fix everything all the time, even when Eve just needed someone to listen.

Now our earthly home will turn against us and we against it: tsunamis and smog, cholera and urban sprawl, *adam* and *adamah* brawling in a bout neither will win. From this moment on, we all come from a broken home.

Despite the broken places, bright spots of God's original plan still gleam through the cracks. Beauty still eclipses the mess in flashes of wonder, and we are momentarily blinded and given sight. There are times that we stare into the face of someone we deeply love, or look at the grandeur of the created world, or find that the whispering Spirit of God drowns out the world for just a moment. And the original blueprint of Eden peeks through and finds us.

When I look back through the story of Genesis 3, I can't help but remember a visit to one of my favorite bookstores, a huge two-story edifice that I frequented as often as my bank account would allow.

Down the escalators from the entrance, the lower story is exclusively filled with children's books. Now, I need to confess that I've never quite outgrown children's literature. My mom was a children's librarian while I was growing up, so children's books feel a little bit like childhood friends to me.

I was making a visit to these friends, in the lower level of my favorite bookstore, when I heard a voice call out that was at the same time both unfamiliar and unmistakable. It didn't belong to anyone I knew, but at the first sound of it I recognized both the caller and the one she was calling.

"Timmy," the voice said. "Timothy, where are you?" There in the children's department, somewhere on the other side of a bookshelf, I could clearly hear the sounds of a mother looking for her lost child.

Since I remember getting lost (on purpose) in plenty of bookstores as a kid, the sound of that voice had me smiling to myself just a little as I kept browsing.

"Tim?" the voice continued. It got more concerned, more serious, calling out a variety of names and nicknames until finally it reached for the one name that can be uttered only by the one who gave it to you. Three names, actually: "Timothy Allen Johnson! You come out right now!"

Soon I found that I was looking for Timmy, too. In fact, when I looked around, every customer on that floor seemed to be searching for him. We didn't know what he looked like, but we were looking under tables and deep into lower bookshelves for a child we had never seen, a search party undeputized but vigilant.

After a little while, word began to spread that little Timothy Allen Johnson was only two-and-a-half years old, a very small fugitive to be separated from his mother for so long. As

I watched helplessly, the look on her face and the sound of her voice became more and more strained and worried because it was becoming clear that we had scoured the whole lower level—and he wasn't there. I followed that mother's gaze up to the big escalators in the center of the store, the only pathway up to the exit. I could almost read her thoughts: *could someone so small have made it up the escalator on his own unnoticed?* And then the thought no one ever wants to think: *what if he hadn't been on his own?*

A clerk brought our search to a more official capacity. He and the mother walked to the desk at the center of the department, and he grabbed the phone that was sitting there to make the urgent call upstairs—the call no one wants to make—to tell them to seal off the exits. But just as the clerk lifted that phone, I watched his eyes look straight in my direction, then past me, and land on something behind me near the back wall of the store. And before he could ever dial he put down the receiver.

When I turned around I saw what he saw: the elevator doors on the back wall opened, and there, crumpled in a little ball in the corner of the elevator, was Timothy Allen Johnson.

Two-year-olds like to push buttons, and when he pushed this one, the magic doors opened, and he went in. The doors closed, and he had been there listening to the chorus of voices call his name all along.

I have never seen a mother move that fast in my life. She sprinted to the elevator, scooped him up, and I was close enough to hear her call out one last name. Actually, she almost whispered it.

"You stinker," she said. "You stinker, you scared Mama. Don't you do that again."

When those first humans made a mess of creation, when they took The Leap, The Fall, The Jump away from following God, they were pretty worried about how God would react. They even went so far as to try to hide from God in the garden he had created. And when God missed them, he went searching, went looking for them. He began calling out to them. There were a lot of things God could have yelled.

How dare you?

I told you so!

What have you done?

But instead God's voice came as clearly through the foliage as if it had been just on the other side of a bookshelf: "Where are you?" (Genesis 3:9)

Where are you? Sound familiar?

"Timmy? Timothy, where are you?"

God's gentleness with his fallen children, guilty and shamed and hiding from him (as if one could hide from God), is the voice of a parent calling out to a lost and hurting child.

There have been times in my life when, wandering and lost, I have heard the voice of God calling to me. I wonder about the times he called and I did not hear. I wonder how he is calling me even today, to return from a lostness I am not even yet wholly aware of. I wonder how he is calling to you. I wonder what would happen if we stopped to hear, and if we could finally respond.

CHAPTER 3

A Family Manifesto
Chosen

I HAVE A SLIGHT OBSESSION WITH office supplies. My desk drawers are a hodgepodge of color-coordinated highlighters and overflowing nests of rubber bands. No matter how great my stock of markers, erasers, and clips I have stored up, I still seem to find an excuse to wander down the office-supply aisle at the store. I swoon a little when I get to the Post-it Notes. The array of colors and sizes (gigantic wall-sized ones! Cute little tiny ones!) makes me crave extra drawer space to hold more notes the way some people covet designer shoes. At least my habit is a little less expensive.

The story of how Post-it Notes originated for some reason makes me love them all the more, because they were born from a mishap.

In 1970, a man named Spencer Silver was working in the 3M research laboratories, trying to create a strong adhesive. Silver's formula was supposed to bind things permanently, but it turned out even weaker than what 3M already manufactured. It stuck to objects, but could easily be lifted off. It was super weak instead of super strong. It was a failure.

Do scientists taunt each other for their flops the way athletes do in locker rooms after the game? If so, I'll bet Spencer Silver took a verbal beating back in the lab for his lemon of a glue. Maybe they superglued his test tubes to the rack and laughed when he tried to pick them up. *"Whatsa matter, Silver? Sticky situation?"* Still, he didn't discard the formula. He filed it away hoping it might have a future.

Then four years later, on a Sunday morning, another 3M scientist named Arthur Fry was singing in his church choir. He had multiple slips of paper sticking out of his hymnal as bookmarks, but they kept falling out of the book. Here's my favorite part: when *his mind wandered during the sermon* (see how God can use even a bad sermon for good?), he started thinking of solutions for his bookmark problem. Remembering Silver's adhesive, Arthur Fry decided to try using some of the failed formula to coat his bookmarks. Suddenly it was a success! With the weak adhesive, the markers stayed in place yet lifted off without damaging the pages, and he found every hymn without missing a beat. Ten years after Silver developed the super weak adhesive, 3M began distributing Post-it Notes nationwide in 1980.[1] They became a huge commercial success and even continue to gain popularity in today's age of technological innovation. No one needs to go to a half-day corporate training to learn how to use Post-it Notes. They never need a system upgrade. When the server goes down or the power goes out, they continue to stick it out.

I don't want to cast disparagement on God's role as inventor of the universe, but you have to agree that at least one of his first ideas didn't start out with much promise. One of my favorite preachers, John Ortberg (minds don't wander during his sermons!), once talked about a conversation God might have had before human beings ever appeared, when most of the earth was still in its research-and-development phase.

Even with all the great things God had created so far, when he had the next idea lined up, for some reason it thrilled him most of all. So he gathered the hosts of angels around and announced his newest invention: the family. He explains that small, helpless beings (children) will be taken on and cared for by large beings (parents). These children will be lots of trouble. They will cry, scream, make messes, talk back, and generally make life difficult. The parents will be irritable and sleep-deprived for years. And then just when the children begin to be self-sufficient and interesting, they will move away.

The angels are hesitant to tell God what they really think. Has he lost his mind? Who's going to want to volunteer for such a thing? None of them wants to tell God their opinion. Ortberg imagines them looking down at their feet and thinking, "Who's going to tell him? I don't want to tell him."

But no one could talk God out of it. Because, as God pointed out, when the grown-ups get to hold this little stranger for the first time, they will say things like, "I never thought I could love anything so much." "He's just so perfect." "She's just so beautiful."

And one day that tiny mouth will smile at them for the first time and they will melt.

They're going to love that little person even though it has never done one thing to deserve it. And even when it's old enough to do exactly what they told it not to do, they're going to love it even more, and forgive it, and give it another chance and another and another, because that's what having a family is about: to have people who will always love you enough to give you another chance.

"And then one day," God says, "when the human race has experienced enough and learned enough from my invention, I'll finally reveal its purpose. I'm going to lean down and whisper to them, 'Guess what? This is how I feel about you, only better. I am YOUR father.'

"And hopefully something is going to click—and they'll finally get it. How much I love them. And they're going to be blown away by the idea that I could love them that much and more. This may seem like a strange way to get through to them, but it's the only way they'll ever get it, ever realize how loved they are, if they experience it here on earth first."

And so God made families. Actually he started with one.

God made a family.

And everything was perfect. And everyone loved each other and spoke respectfully to each other in dulcet tones and picked up their socks off the floor the first time they were asked. And they all lived happily ever after.

Right?

Actually, God made the very first family, and that's when

things started to go wrong. The angels must have looked at what he had done and said, "God, there's something flawed in your invention. Actually, I think it's broken."

Because with the very first family came the very first family fight. Eve ate a piece of fruit and shared it with her husband, Adam, and God showed up and asked them, "What happened here?"

And Adam said, "Well God, this woman that you gave me...she gave me the fruit! So I ate it."

Ortberg says, "Only one other human being in the whole world and the man blames her and you notice he does not even call her by name." Don't you love that? Not *Eve* gave me the fruit. Not my *wife* gave me the fruit. No. The woman! The woman that YOU put here with me.[2]

We do the same thing, don't we?

You'll never guess what YOUR SON did today?

Or you go tell YOUR MOTHER to take care of it.

This woman that you gave me, Adam says. She was your idea, God. Not mine.

Shame—dark, deep, and deadly—has crept into the human heart. We'll put on the mask of blaming others it won't be enough. We'll try to cover it up with fig leaves, but they won't quite stretch to fit. We'll resort to whining, deceiving, denying, acting out, passive-aggressive behavior, and emotional eating, but none of them are going to fix our shame problem.

By the next generation, sin has mushroomed from fruit picking to homicide. Cain and Abel are proof that if we don't learn from our mistakes in one generation, things just get worse.

The story of the first sibling relationship is also the story of the first murder.

I'm convinced that ever since that second generation, parenting siblings has mostly been about preventing another Cain and Abel.

When my husband, Jim, and his older sister, Ann, were growing up, they would spend a few weeks each summer visiting grandparents. Like most children, they looked forward to the fun visit and special treatment they received during those weeks. The grandparents looked forward to spoiling their grandchildren. It's not until you have kids yourself that you realize that the biggest reason for grandparent visits is really the generation in the middle—giving the exhausted parents a break!

The funny thing to me about these stories they tell of summer visits to their grandparents' is that neither child ever stayed with the same grandparents at the same time. Ann would be dropped off to visit one set of grandparents, and Jim would visit the others. Then, halfway through their visit, the grandparents would meet up and swap kids.

You could make up some great reasons for these visits in isolation: individual attention for the kids, aging grandparents who might be worn out from too much noise and activity, but the true reason for their segregation was Cain and Abel. Their parents were sure that if you left two kids at one house for the week, you might just have one left to pick up at the end. Their parents were sure they would kill each other!

The story of Cain and Abel actually explains a lot about siblings and their tumultuous relationships for the rest of time.

So far we're only to the second generation and this invention isn't working so well. At one point, just six chapters into Genesis, things go completely south.

"The LORD saw that humanity had become thoroughly evil on the earth and that every idea their minds thought up was always completely evil" (Genesis 6:5).

Instead of one or two bad apples, the language about the depravity of the human race includes words like *every, only,* and *all.*

It gets so bad that the chaos created by *adam* (the people) is so complete that its effects ricochet through their *adama,* their earthly home. The order God set about creating in the very beginning by separating the water above and the water below is reversed, and chaos streams in from every direction.

"On that day all the springs of the deep sea erupted, and the windows in the skies opened. It rained on the earth forty days and forty nights" (Genesis 7:11-12).

Almost the entire human experiment gets flushed, and God decides to reboot creation. He starts over with what seems to be just one perfect family: Noah and his sons and their wives.

The illustrated children's Bible that sat in the waiting room of my dentist's office when I was a child was always a fascination for me. Flipping through it made for a great distraction from the dreaded future that awaited me past the exam room door. After the scandalous picture of a naked Adam and Eve (standing behind strategic foliage, Eve's long hair carefully arranged for a G rating), I loved to look at the pictures of Noah loading up the ark, his long white beard flowing behind him in the wind while the cute animals processed two by two up the plank. It didn't ever show the crowds of people being covered by the rising water, their hands frantically reaching upward as the flood overtook them. We're just not sure what to do with that part of the story.

Noah and family are the righteous remnants of this dark chapter of Genesis, the seeming *Leave It to Beaver* bunch out of a mob not worth saving. You'd think the earth would get off to a better start this time with such model citizens, but right after they step off the boat, Noah gets drunk. (He is a vintner after all, surrounded by fields full of temptation. How can we expect him to do better than the couple who only had to stay away from one tree?) One of his sons sees him naked and mocks his inebriated dad, bringing a curse on all his descendants. And *this* is supposed to be the most righteous family of their generation. It sounds like the bar may have been set kind of low.

Finally, Genesis reaches this kind of low point in chapter 11. It's the absolute moral bankruptcy of the human family. (I like to think that's why they put it in chapter 11—the bankruptcy chapter.)

This time, the people haven't just turned on each other, they've turned on God. People have gotten so bad that their goal is to replace God, to kick God off the throne of the universe and climb high enough that they themselves will be gods now. This isn't really a new temptation. Even their Edenic ancestors were putting themselves in God's place by striking his rules and making their own.

But this time it's universal. Instead of individual, it's corporate. Instead of private, it's global. Sin is a virus and no one is immune. The more they communicate, the more it spreads. So God scatters them about by mixing up their language. And the tower they were trying to build gets nicknamed the Tower of Babel.

They have lost their ability to truly communicate. And so when you look into the eyes of your wife, your weird brother-in-law, your teenage daughter, and think something like, *I just can't understand you!* This is who you have to thank. The good people of chapter 11.

If anyone ever wanted to say, "We told you so" to God, it was probably those angels watching the deterioration on earth in that moment. They had predicted from the beginning that the creation of people was a risky investment, that this experiment called the human family was probably doomed from the start.

But instead of discouraged or defeated, God gets the most excited we've seen him so far at the end of chapter 11. Because here he rolls his sleeves up and gets ready to turn the page to chapter 12. Chapter 12 of Genesis is where God unveils his secret weapon: something he says will fix everything, turn it all around, restore the world to the way he wanted it to be in the very beginning.

I'm sure the angels were peering over his shoulder, curious, nosy, dying to see what this amazing secret weapon could be. It would have to be something amazing. Something incredible. Something big. God doesn't really have any small ideas, right?

When we turn the page from the bankruptcy chapter of the Bible, chapter 11, the page where humanity sank to one of its lowest points, and we open to chapter 12, do you know what God's amazing secret weapon is?

A family. That's it. God made a family. That's the secret weapon he wants to use to save the world. No grandiose display of power or might, no new technology or contraptions.

When God wanted to change the world, he started with a family. Their names were Abraham and Sarah, and God promised them he would bless them beyond their wildest dreams. But the blessing wasn't for them to keep. They were going to be blessed to be a blessing.

This is the Post-it Note moment for God's invention of family—the moment the world would realize that the seemingly fragile bond created in Eden would prove to be an ingenious formula, tucked into the recesses of creation until the moment it would change everything.

The blessing God would pour out into Abraham and Sarah's family would overflow to restore the rest of God's broken world. You would think, with a job that big, that this would be the family that would finally get it right. That this, finally, would be the perfect family.

But even this family is far from perfect. In fact, Abraham and Sarah and their kids and their grandkids have a lot of problems. They have the same problems families had before and since. Because there is no such thing as the perfect family.

Sometimes when we're sitting in church, and the sermon mentions something about families, I can actually see people sliding down in their seats a little. Sometimes when churches start talking about families, people who are divorced or childless or widowed or never married feel left out. That definitely isn't God's plan.

Sometimes people think, because their family has issues, they don't really belong with all these other people at church. Because our family has a rift in it, or a secret, or because there's been alcoholism or abuse, because somebody had a baby when they weren't supposed to, or couldn't have a baby when they wanted to, or someone's not speaking to someone else, or somebody got remarried once, or twice, or ten times, or maybe just because our sweet little family that was holding hands while walking into church in our coordinating outfits on Sunday morning was screaming at one other in the van in the parking lot five minutes earlier.

Maybe when they start talking about families in church they aren't really talking to us, because we don't have the perfect family.

Do you know what it means if you don't have the perfect family? If your family fits one of those descriptions, or maybe they have something else going on that you're embarrassed to even name? Do you know what it means if your family's abnormal, atypical, imperfect?

Welcome to the family. We're all in the same boat.

If God could've chosen the perfect family to be his secret weapon to change the world, he probably would've. But there was no perfect family available. There still isn't. But that didn't mean God gave up on families. He knew they were just too important.

Families are what God invented to show us how he feels about us. He knew we would need human contact to get it, that we would only understand God's love because someone with skin on loved us first. We only understand forgiveness and grace and unconditional love from God if we experience it first embodied in person. And because family is such an important idea, when families mess up, God doesn't give up on them. He keeps loving, keeps trying, keeps offering grace again and again. And that's what we're supposed to do for each other too.

When Abraham and Sarah got their divine call to be God's secret weapon, the family that saved the world, they didn't always get things right. But God never gave up on them. Their family grew and generations passed, until finally, God's plan became clear—just how this secret weapon was going to work. Because into their family, in a generation no more perfect than any other, God sent his own Son.

The Gospel of John introduces Jesus' arrival with these words: "The Word became flesh and made his dwelling among us. We have seen his glory, the glory of the one and only Son, who came from the Father, full of grace and truth" (John 1:14 NIV).

The literal description of "made his dwelling" is from the Greek word that means "to pitch a tent." Jesus came and pitched his tent among us here on earth. He took up residence in our camp, in a tent made of flesh and blood. God looked down at this family filled with wonderful, weird, crazy people, and chose to make his Son their son. He put on a tent of their DNA, of our flesh, and helped us understand just how serious he is about this family business.

God could've shown up on earth in any way that he wanted (surfing in on a tsunami? Parachuting in from the beyond?), but he considered families important enough that he chose to be born in one.

That means Jesus can trace his ancestry back to Abraham and Sarah and all their dysfunctional crew, back to Noah and his backward sons, back to those people in moral bankruptcy at Babel, all the way back to Adam and Eve and the mess that started it all.

Jesus is the ultimate branch of this family that God chose to change the world. Know who else is part of this family?

The letter to the Galatians puts it this way: "And now that you belong to Christ, you are the true children of Abraham. You are his heirs, and God's promise to Abraham belongs to you" (Galatians 3:29 NLT).

God invites us into this crazy, special family called by God to be his secret weapon to change the world. He made room for you, for me. We belong.

And this family, which has been called a lot of things over time—the Chosen People, the Sons of Abraham, the Nation of Israel—is now called one final thing: the church. The place where everyone, absolutely everyone, is invited to be part of the family.

The special assignment of families is to be a place for people to learn love, grace, and acceptance from people on earth so that we can grasp how God really loves them. But there are some people who didn't receive that kind of message from the family they grew up in. Frankly, they got exactly the opposite: criticism, condemnation, rejection.

So God made a new kind of family, the church, and assigned us the task of showing people what that kind of love looks like. He wants the family of faith to offer love so warm and real and inviting that people can understand, can see the love of an unseen God.

When God opens up the definition of family to include all of us who have faith in Christ, it means that God's secret weapon of blessing just got a lot bigger. Those who have been tuning out of the family conversation, thinking they aren't part of the conversation because they aren't "raising a family"—because they are empty nesters or in their golden years or never married or don't have kids—suddenly find themselves thrust right into the center of the action.

Because hidden in plain sight all around us are those who desperately need a surrogate mom, some grandfatherly wisdom, the influence of a strong father figure, a sister in Christ, someone who will become like a daughter or a son to them.

These are people who won't know how much they are loved unless we tell them, unless we show them.

We can probably all name a list of people who have been messengers of divine love for us, who helped us understand that we were worth caring for. What's harder is to identify the other list: the people that are being given to us so that we might love, mentor, and influence them. Celebrating those who have loved us is easy. Believing that we are capable of being that kind of force in someone else's life takes more effort. But the effort is worth it. If we can believe that we are the ones God is using to introduce his love to others, we can become part of the most powerful force the world has ever known. What changes the world? A family. And this family belongs to God.

There's this thing we do in Christian circles where we talk about God having a purpose for each of us, this call to action where we challenge people to do something "really important" with their life. Something that matters in God's kingdom.

I've seen the light bulb go on in so many people's eyes about the important work they're being called to do for God's kingdom. I've seen wealthy doctors leave their jobs and become missionaries in developing countries. I've seen people begin spending each weekend in prison to help communicate God's love behind bars. I've watched people start nonprofits that took on major diseases and societal problems. All because they heard and answered the call to begin doing God's "important work."

But sometimes when I hear a message like that, calling

people to do something really significant with their lives, I think of those people I know who are spending or have spent much of their time and energy and sweat and tears on families. Sometimes the families they're tending are their children or parents or siblings. And sometimes they are tending the family they find in church or in community.

When I think of the people I know who are truly changing the world for God, I think of those who are investing in multiple generations either of their own family or of those at church, of the teachers who treat the children that pass through their classroom like their own because there is such a desperate need for nurture as well as education, of the parents whose house becomes the gathering place of all the children in the neighborhood because they are a safe and warm place to land. I think of all the parents and grandparents who put family first over their own needs again and again. Maybe you're one of them. Maybe you are one of those unsung saints who is changing the world, answering this calling to go above and beyond and do something really important with your life for God's kingdom. Or maybe you are someone who is being called, right now, tugged by God to tend more directly to your church family or your home family.

The family is not some place to go at the end of the day when our important work is done. It is our important work.

It's not just a landing place from all of the really significant things that happen in the outside world. It is the most significant thing we could invest your lives in.

Family is God's best idea. His favorite invention. It's his

way of communicating his love and grace through human arms and acceptance, because the only way people will know how an invisible God loves them is if we love them first. Big or small, little kids or aging parents, people related by blood or people bound by the family opened to us all by Jesus Christ and our Abba Father. This is where God's secret weapon is at work, where his invention is working at its best.

As small as it seems, that's all there is to it: the earth-shaking, world-changing invention we call family. This is our most important work.

CHAPTER 4

Abraham and Sarah
Control

WE INHERIT SO MUCH MORE THAN pianos and armoires from our families Anyone who has ever heard their own words followed by the thought, *I sound just like my mother!* knows just how deeply we carry with us the furnishings of the family in which we grew up. Some of those pieces are lovely, admirable things. Others are destructive, bitter, bequeathed through the generations by simple force of habit. Families are constructed to be the machine that forms us, that makes us who we are. Whether we like the results or not, it's tough to deny that the machine works.

It's not a bad idea to examine our emotional furniture from time to time—to see where it came from and whether it's worth keeping. Without reflection and intentionality, the characteristics we've inherited will be the same ones we pass down, whether to our own flesh and blood families or to any others who get close enough for us to affect in a relationship.

There is some kind of inspiration in that—looking back

in order to look forward, sorting through our things before they're transferred to the next generation.

That makes me think of Sarah. Sweet Sarah. She may not have realized that she was a link in a chain of people passing things down generation to generation. Sometimes Sarah wondered if there would even be a next generation. She and her husband, Abraham, had been promised by God that their descendants would be as numerous as the stars, but as of yet, not even one little nova had appeared in their family constellation. Still, God chose this aging pair (still childless in their sixties and seventies) to be the recipients of a promise that would know no borders: "I will make of you a great nation and will bless you. I will make your name respected, and you will be a blessing. I will bless those who bless you, those who curse you I will curse; all the families of the earth will be blessed because of you" (Genesis 12:2-3).

The unusual nature of the promise declared that they would be the vessel through which God would pour blessing to all the peoples on earth. They were to be conduits, not containers, of the immense goodness of God. This strategy, the contagious blessing spread by one family, became the means through which God would make this family his secret weapon to restore the world.

When God wants to change the world, he starts with a family...

There is no way to overstate what a countercultural, shocking idea this would have been at the time, that one family would reach out to bless others. Society in Abraham's and

Sarah's day was centered around family as a unit in ways we have a hard time comprehending. Nuclear families lived bonded together in clans and tribes with their relatives. If one clan's interests were threatened, or if someone else competed for its resources, that clan would do all in its power—even go to war—to protect their own.

The idea that our goal should be to just take care of our own, even at the expense of others, has outlasted humanity's practice of living in tribes. Those looking to protect the interests of their own "tribe" have instigated battles around dinner tables, between gangs, even between world powers. Abraham's and Sarah's offspring would be called the chosen people because of their unique arrangement with God. But when they began to forget that they were chosen for a purpose, contracted for a specific vocation, they too would miss the point of the outward-focused mission for which God had chosen them. As part of this family line, you and I are destined to struggle with the same kind of choice: Do we keep what is "ours" for our own sake, or do we recognize that all good things come from above—not only to our hands but also through them and to the hands of others?

God's promise of immense blessing to Abraham and Sarah was not without cost. They were called to pick up and leave everything they knew and go to a place they did not know. "The LORD said to Abram, "Leave your land, your family, and your father's household for the land that I will show you" (Genesis 12:1).

God's list of what they must leave behind was so specific,

and the destination so vague. I wonder if they longed for an address, a set of GPS coordinates, even just a more detailed description of this wonderful land that God promised. But this calling to go, to leave, contained what would be their major contribution to this divine connection: trust. God would provide the place, the people, his presence, and protection. They would just need to trust.

It sounds so easy, doesn't it? Just trust God. It's the kind of phrase we embroider on throw pillows and hang on our refrigerators. But when God calls us to leave the visible and journey toward the invisible unknown, something in us always resists. We cling to what we know. We struggle to let go of control and grab hold of trust, like a trapeze bar just out of reach. Somehow clinging to the reins of control, no matter what a mess we make of things, seems preferable to trusting the unknown plan that God has in mind. Abraham's and Sarah's story is a constant struggle to decide where the pendulum will swing between those two poles. Just trust God. It's not as easy as it sounds. Just ask Sarah.

Somewhere along the way, Sarah began to have doubts. It wasn't that she thought this God they were following would fail to keep his promises, it was just that he seemed to need a little help. God wasn't delivering on his promise to answer her heart's desire for children within the timetable Sarah thought he should have, and so she decided to help him along a little bit. I *know the plans I have for me, God, she seemed to say. Plans to prosper me and not to harm me. Plans to give me a hope and a future. Let me just give your plan a little nudge.*

Sarah's solution was to enlist her maid, Hagar, to serve as a surrogate mother. *Surely* this *is what you meant, God....This waiting is getting us nowhere.* Here's how we know how desperate Sarah has become: with no fertility clinics, no artificial insemination, no in vitro fertilization, giving her maid to her husband means exactly what it sounds like—getting her pregnant the old-fashioned way. Sarah sent her maid into her husband's bed. Hagar became a surrogate, carrying a baby that Abraham and Sarah raised as their own. This kind of arrangement wasn't unheard of at the time. Slaves were persons without rights or status—Hagar was a tool to be used and discarded, whether for her work or her womb.

What happens next shouldn't come as much of a surprise. The new arrangement couldn't have been comfortable for Sarah, and the unpleasantness didn't end when her plan succeeded and Hagar's waistline began to expand. Just picture how awkward life must have been in the home of the expectant trio.

Hagar's pregnancy was her first taste of importance; she had been unnoticed for a long time. The baby within her outranked her and brought with it the weight of status. As Hagar's belly grew, so did her attitude. Maybe she began to drop things and asked Sarah to pick them up for her. Maybe she held her aching back until Sarah felt obliged to clean the floor and let her rest. Maybe Abraham stepped in, saying, "Hagar's not feeling well tonight, Sarah. Would you make her a nice dinner?" Sarah seethed with irritation and anger, so she began to retaliate, making Hagar's life miserable.

Despondent, Hagar fled the home that was once a haven and ran away into the desert. The plan that began with Sarah's desperation is now mirrored in Hagar's: you know a pregnant woman is desperate if she intentionally flees into a sweltering climate while great with child.

There in the desert, dejected and alone, Hagar heard the voice of God calling to her. Hagar is a slave, a foreigner, a runaway, but as insignificant as she is to everyone else, she is significant to God. She is the one lost sheep, and the Shepherd continues the search he began in Eden for his lost children: *Where are you?* While the story of Genesis is primarily about one family, a "chosen people," they are chosen to be part of God's search and rescue mission. Hagar is living proof that God searches for all of us, no matter our status or nationality. No matter if we feel chosen or outcast. Each person matters to God, otherwise he would leave the castoffs in the desert to die.

When Hagar returned from the frying pan back to the fire of a hostile climate at home, she fulfilled her part of the contract and gave birth to the offspring of Sarah's plan, but the problems had only begun. A household made up of a daddy and a mommy and a mommy—and a baby makes four—made for a complicated arrangement indeed. And when, fourteen years later, the alarm finally went off on Sarah's biological clock, and she gave birth to the long-awaited baby Isaac, things only got worse.

At last, Sarah cradled her answered prayer in her arms, but there was one thing that kept her from enjoying the moment. Ishmael was a constant reminder of her lack of trust in

God's plan. His presence was a black spot on her perfect and complete family portrait: competition for her own bouncing baby boy. A quick search into the history of almost any royal family will confirm what Sarah already knew: two rival heirs in the same house means disaster for one of them. So Sarah did what she knew best—she took control again. A new sin was birthed to erase the two unwanted figures from the family portrait. She schemed a second, horrifying plan to erase the effects of her first, commanding her husband to dispose of them. "Get rid of that slave woman and her son, for that woman's son will never share in the inheritance with my son Isaac" (Genesis 21:10 NIV).

Cast out into the desert to die, Hagar found herself wandering in familiar territory with her teenage son at her side. This time it's not by choice. This time there's no home to return to, no family to welcome them back. This time the water runs out with no rescue in sight, and it looked likely that they would both die in the desert. When hope ran out, too, she left Ishmael, delirious from heat and dehydration, in the shade of a bush and stumbled away, unable to watch her only son die.

> Then she went off and sat down about a bowshot away, for she thought, "I cannot watch the boy die." And as she sat there, she began to sob. God heard the boy crying, and the angel of God called to Hagar from heaven and said to her, "What is the matter, Hagar? Do not be afraid; God has heard the boy crying as he lies there." (Genesis 21:16-17 NIV)

Hagar sobbed, wailed, cried out a deep concern for the child she loved with all of her heart. And God heard and responded, but specifically, he answered Ishmael's cries. In response to her loud wailing, Hagar is told, "God heard your son."

Hagar is the Bible's first single mother. The struggles she confronted are not so different from those who feel sole responsibility for someone they love today. She felt abandoned and alone as she shouldered the heavy responsibility of making a life and a future for her son. She would have given anything, including her own life, to be sure that he lived.

The way God let her know that he had listened to and heard Ishmael is a gentle reminder that she was not the only one who cared for the boy. She was not the only one responsible for his welfare and his future. No matter how she loved him, she couldn't control his future. No matter how she worried, she couldn't save him. God reminded her that he heard Ishmael so that she would know that God is the one who can save. For those of us who have felt deep concern for someone we love—a child, a spouse, a family member, or friend—Hagar's story assures us that we can never out-love God. Her story tells us that when we see and hear the troubled lives of our loved ones, God sees and hears. God cares. Giving up control of those we love to him in prayer is the best thing we can do for them and for us.

Hagar's two trips to the desert are similar in their stories of desperation, an estrangement encounter with a saving God. But they differ in ending. The first time she ran to the desert, God brought rescue by bringing her out and returning her safely home. The second time, God moved in and made a home for Hagar and her son in the wasteland. Instead of moving them out, God moves in.

The desert is a place most of us will visit at one time or another. When we find ourselves in desert times, we may ask God to rescue us from the desert, but he may choose to move in and make the desert bloom.

It happens when we least expect it—the experience of feeling forgotten, abandoned, unwanted, or depressed. If you're going through a desert time in your life, I pray that you, like Hagar, will experience some of your most vivid encounters with God in the desert.

Easy circumstances are no proof of God's blessing. Difficult ones are no indication of his absence. As you travel in and out of the desert seasons of your life, remember that God travels with you. You are never alone. And if you're praying for a loved one who seems to be wandering in a desert of their own, it's good to know that God sees, God hears, God cares, and God can make a desert bloom.

In the desert, Hagar learns that no matter how much she loves her son, she will never love him more than God loves him. She can never guarantee his safety or control his future.

Back at home, Sarah learns that the future she tried so hard to manipulate was in God's hands all along. No matter how many times Sarah grabbed the reins of the situation, God showed again and again that he is the one in control. No amount of plotting can derail his plans.

Sarah didn't make this up on her own. She inherited it. It's part of Eve's legacy, the hand-me-downs of this family's Fall (or Leap) from grace.

When Adam and Eve were still standing in their newly realized naked state, discarded cores from the forbidden fruit still scattered fresh on the dirt by the forbidden tree, the consequences of what they had done began to dawn on them. Part of Eve's consequence was this: "You will desire your husband, but he will rule over you" (Genesis 3:16).

The desire God is speaking of is not a good kind of desire—God isn't just saying Eve will long for Adam to get home when he's been out of town on a business trip. God is saying she will want to control, to manipulate.

In the very first generation, "Eve listened to the voice of the serpent." In Abraham's and Sarah's case, we're told, "Abram listened to the voice of Sarai" (Genesis 16:2 NRSV). Sarah, it turns out, was following in the footsteps of a snake (if a snake had footsteps!). The role she took on was the role of one who pushed a family away from God's plan and toward her own desires, one who manipulated and controlled. It's a role many of us know all too well.

There is within us a very human desire to control and manipulate, and to force things to get what we want. And even when we do get what we want, we usually find that things don't turn out so great in the end. Everything about the entrance of Hagar and her son Ishmael into the family story was a disaster. And yet it's there in all of us, whether we like it or not—the desire to play God for the people we love. It's there somewhere in you. It's within me, too.

That unwanted part of my own personality became abundantly clear to me the year of my ultimate breakup. Ultimate breakup stories usually trump other relationship memories in drama and collateral damage, but mine was ultimate not only in magnitude but in timing, since it was my last breakup—the end of the relationship with the last person I dated a few years before I met my husband, Jim.

This opposites-attract romance had been fun for a while— Brent was the outgoing, magnetic big-man-on-campus. I was the more bookish one people sought out for deep conversation. But fun seemed to be as deep as our connection went. I thought we could both see that it was going nowhere, that he'd probably nod in agreement and we'd most likely shake hands and walk away friends. I was in for a surprise. During our relationship Brent had been all jokes and fun—no serious side to be seen. The minute we broke up, an entirely different side of his personality emerged. He cried. He moped. This person who had been the life of the party was suddenly in a terrible mood all over the very small graduate school campus where we were both students. Because of the fishbowl of a community we lived in, it was impossible for me to escape the breakup. If I went to classes, he was there. In the chapel, he was there crying and praying at the altar. In the library, he was there being comforted by one of our very close-knit group of shared friends.

I began to feel like the world's biggest jerk.

Eventually, when our friends wanted to get together, they

were faced with the decision of which one of us to invite. It's not much fun to have people over when two of them are off in different corners sulking. Awkward and uncomfortable are not fun party guests. I started to feel paranoid about losing my friends. Paranoid that they were all meeting somewhere and inviting him instead of me. Paranoid they would take his side and think I was a terrible person for breaking his heart. Eventually an unofficial custody agreement began to develop: I got some friends in the separation while he got others. What I thought would be an easy, mutual breakup ended up being one of the most painful experiences of my life.

My one safety net through the whole ordeal was my best friend, who was also my roommate. I had poured out my heart to her about the whole sordid situation. There was a sort of unspoken agreement that since she was my best friend she would only talk to me—not to him—even though they had become good friends as well. I didn't have to worry that she would include him and not me in some event or get together. I didn't have to worry she would take his side over mine. That's the definition of a best friend—she was mine, not his. She belonged to me.

One day I heard some gossip about my ex on campus. He had asked another girl out on a date. (Not my best friend. This is not *that* kind of story.) This was big news. A breakup breakthrough. That elusive thing all breakers-up grasp for: closure. Part of me was excited—maybe now we could both get on with our lives. But, to be honest, part of me didn't want him to move on. It wasn't that I wanted him, it was that

I realized part of me wanted to be difficult to get over—wanted him to be miserable forever, because that would be a clear sign of just how great I really was.

I rushed home to tell my best friend, but when I ran into her room and blurted out the news she got a funny look on her face. Not the dropped jaw of surprise I had expected. So I stopped in my tracks and asked her what was going on.

She explained carefully that she had known for over a week. That he had told her. Then the kicker—that they had been meeting every week since the breakup so that *he* could talk about *his* feelings.

"He needed a friend," she said apologetically.

I couldn't believe it! My own best friend! She was *my* friend, not his! How dare she talk to him! She was mine. She belonged to *me*, not him.

This was the worst. Out of the whole breakup, this was the moment that hit me like a kick in the gut. I couldn't figure out why the ongoing fallout of this relationship was affecting me so deeply. I just couldn't shake it. So I decided to go to counseling to try to figure it out.

Let me just stop and say that I think counseling is a gift from God. If I get to a point where I'm physically sick and I can't figure out how to heal something that's wrong with my body, I go to the doctor. When I get to a point where I don't have the resources to figure out what's going on with me emotionally, I go to a counselor.

I sat down in my first visit to this counselor and didn't even give her a chance to talk. I just blurted it all out: How much I'd been struggling with this breakup, even though it didn't seem like it had been all that serious. How all of our friends seemed split between us, almost like a custody battle where we had to figure out when we could each spend time with them. Then I told her how the worst part of the story was that my own best friend, whom I owned, had been fraternizing with the enemy all along. I think I may have used names like Judas or Benedict Arnold, but I can't be sure.

It was at this point, when I finally took a breath, that the counselor finally had a chance to speak. And when she did she said the most awful thing to me.

She said, "It's hard when we can't control people, isn't it?"

I was stunned. What was I supposed to say to that? She was making it sound like *I* had a problem. I thought I was there to talk about *them* and *their* problems. I was the victim here. Right?

And then she started to ask me about my family. (As if they had anything to do with this.) She gently asked about my parents' divorce when I was less than a year old, and about how they each remarried and redivorced before I was in middle school. She asked about the custody agreement where I had to go back and forth from my mom during the week to my dad on alternating weekends, and how with every trip I felt pulled between them.

She asked how it felt to be a little child who had to realize that grown-ups can come in and out of your life—that people who cared about you could leave you anytime they wanted to.

And that even though you were a little kid, you were expected to handle it, to make whomever you were with feel like you loved them the best, like they were the one who owned you.

And suddenly the story I was telling cracked open. It was no longer just about something that had happened in the last year of my life. It was also about something that had been going on a lot longer, something that had begun decades ago and was really about my family and where I came from. It was about the script I had inherited and was still playing parts from, even though the other characters had changed.

It was about how feeling out of control can make you want to control everything you can, especially the people you love.

It is hard when we can't control people, isn't it? It's hard when people don't do the things we think they should.

It's hard when the people we love don't move in the direction we think they should as quickly as we'd like them to. It's hard when our spouses or parents or siblings just won't change in ways we see that they need to. It's hard when our kids, either as children or adults, don't follow the dreams we've dreamed for them.

When we can't seem to make people behave the way we want them to, it becomes harder and harder not to be in control. The more we love people the harder it is. The problem with this desire to control people's actions is that it makes us very anxious and worried, because when people won't do what we want them to do, there's no telling how things will turn out.

This desire to control things has a long pedigree—it reaches back to the earliest families in the Bible. What I keep noticing in my own life is that if I don't notice, and refuse to act on, this deep-seated need to manipulate things to get them to go my way, I'm going to hand it down to those that I love. If we find ourselves caught up in directing the paths of those who are gifts in our lives, rather than sending our petitions for their future to the Giver, it's time to stop. Just stop. And reorient ourselves again to examine our place in the creation, to praise the One who created, to remember that we are not God, and be thankful for the One who was and is and will be always.

When I find myself in the passenger's seat of our car, about to take on the role of "driving instructor" for my husband, who has been driving longer than I have...when I see my toddler struggle to "do it herself" when I could do it faster...when the course of the life of someone I love has taken a turn that I would not choose...I try to whisper to myself, "Be still. Be still and know that I am God." Then I find, once again with all thankfulness, that he is and that I am not.

There's a motivation whispered back from future generations. If our pain isn't transformed, it will end up transferred. The next bequest, I think, is taping a second note next to the first, granting permission, when needed, to throw out the antiques and start fresh.

We inherit so much from our families. I'm grateful for what I've inherited from mine. Those antique pieces sit side by side, old with new, mixed and matched with those I've decided to start new within this generation. The greatest gift of all may be the freedom to redecorate.

CHAPTER 5

Isaac
Cling

OUR LOVED ONES ARE NEVER truly ours. Not in the sense that a car can be ours, or a sweater, or a decorative paperweight. So often, as soon as we claim ownership of those we have been given, we are forced to realize that it is a temporary possession, and one given on loan at that.

Vanessa was proud to claim her little family as her own. Their tidy family existence fit well into her neatly ordered life. Vanessa was a neatnick from an early age. If she said it once a day, she repeated it a dozen times as she picked up after her husband and two small daughters: "Everything has a place and everything in its place." She prided herself on her spotless home and reputation. In a small town where the favorite pastime was talking about other people's families, she made sure that there were only good things to say about her two beautiful and well-behaved little girls. Their family was a fixture at the small Presbyterian church on Sundays, the girls sitting between their parents, often wearing matching dresses and hair bows.

As a teenager, Lauren, the older of the two, began to rebel against her mother's ideas of what it meant to be a proper young lady. She was drawn to tight T-shirts and ripped jeans instead of dresses, and her weekend plans no longer involved church. Still, Vanessa had no idea how far her daughter had strayed from her mother's ideals until she found out that Lauren was pregnant at seventeen.

Vanessa panicked. She was furious with her daughter but at the same time longed to throw her arms around her and tell her it was all going to be OK, like she had when Lauren was a little girl. Somehow the only thing that came out of her mouth was fury, not compassion. *How could you do this to our family?!* She insisted that Lauren spend the duration of her pregnancy at the home of an aunt who lived out of state and then give up the baby for adoption.

Lauren refused, insisting that she wanted to keep the baby. The nightly screaming matches between the two had Vanessa's stomach in knots. None of the parenting books tidily lined up on her shelf had prepared her for this. Finally, the week before Lauren's eighteenth birthday, Vanessa woke to find Lauren's bed still neatly made. She had packed her things and left during the night. She didn't leave a note.

For the next two years, Vanessa had no word from Lauren. She felt like she couldn't show her face in town. Having been part of gossipy conversations about families like her own, she knew exactly what the others were saying. Depressed and angry with God, Vanessa dropped out of her social circles and stopped going to church. Why, when she had followed all the rules, had such a terrible thing happened in her family? She was no longer sure that she even believed in God.

One night, her husband, Wayne, sat her down and said he had something to tell her. Having worried all this time about what had become of Lauren, Vanessa prepared herself for the worst. Instead of bad news, Wayne said that Lauren had contacted him several weeks earlier, inviting him to visit her in a small apartment in the city where she was making a life with her young daughter. Lauren was afraid her mother wouldn't ever consider being part of her life again, so she had asked her dad to reach out on her behalf.

They met at a restaurant that wasn't nearly as nice as those Vanessa was used to frequenting. She sat nervously watching the door, looking for her little girl to come in. She almost didn't recognize the thin young woman carrying a toddler and a diaper bag who entered and sat down at their table. The fierce tension that had bound Vanessa for so long broke when Lauren introduced Libby to her grandmother. Realizing that her own pride had kept her from being part of this sweet little girl's first year and a half of life, Vanessa wept.

The situation was awkward as Vanessa, Wayne, and Lauren went through the motions of looking at menus, placing an order, and making small talk. But when their food arrived, little Libby lifted her hands out to either side of her high chair and babbled as if she were waiting on something. When Vanessa looked to her daughter for an explanation, Lauren grabbed one of Libby's hands and said to her mother, "Mom, she wants us to pray." As she took her granddaughter's hand in her own for the first time and bowed her head, Vanessa felt the hardness of her heart toward the God she had blamed begin to melt away.

Passing faith on to the next generation is a difficult task. No one yet has developed the right list of instructions or the perfect formula to follow that will ensure that those we love will come to recognize and claim for themselves the blessings of the faith we hold so dear.

For Abraham and Sarah in the biblical narrative, any thoughts about the transmission of beliefs to a new genera- tion meant a great longing to have someone who could be an heir to their faith. Almost the entirety of Abraham and Sarah's written story is the story of waiting. A quarter of a century of their story passes while they wait and wonder if God will fulfill his promise to give them a child. If that quarter century was, say, from Abraham's twenty-fifth to fiftieth years, that would be enough to make us take notice. If it spanned the years from his fiftieth to his seventy-fifth birthdays, we would certainly consider it something of a miracle. But God first ap- pears to Abraham when he is seventy-five—so the twenty-five years of waiting and miracle that follows actually deserve to be the cover story of the record books.

The arrival of baby Isaac would be a tabloid sensation in our day. *One-hundred-year-old man and his ninety-year-old wife give birth! Diapers and Depends in one family! World's oldest parents seen pushing a stroller and a walker to the park!* It's little wonder that the baby's name meant "laughter." There was a lot to giggle about when looking at the wrinkled couple and their bouncing baby boy.

When, after more chapters of waiting than any other Biblical story, the Genesis birth announcement finally comes, proclaiming the arrival of Isaac, child of promises kept, we'd expect some fanfare. Instead, Scripture shares the news with these abrupt words.

> She became pregnant and gave birth to a son for Abraham when he was old, at the very time God had told him. Abraham named his son—the one Sarah bore him—Isaac. Abraham circumcised his son Isaac when he was eight days old just as God had commanded him. Abraham was 100 years old when his son Isaac was born. (Genesis 21:2-5)

That's it? We might at least expect them to pass around some cigars. For an announcement we've waited twenty-five years to hear, it's a bit anticlimactic. He was born. He was a boy. They named him. They circumcised him. And Abraham was one hundred years old when it all happened. There's nothing about the baby. Was he cute? Did he have a full head of hair? How much did he weigh? And how is Sarah doing? Abraham's age at the time is impressive, but a ninety-year-old woman just gave birth! At least mention her!

I've always blamed this lack of information on the

conventional history of biblical narrators being, well, male. Men don't often elaborate in announcements like this. When my husband happens to be the first one who gets the news that friends of ours have had their baby, he usually delivers it like this: "They had the baby." No news about the baby's name, the weight, who the baby looks like, or how the mother is doing. Sometimes I even have to prod: "Is it a girl or a boy?" To which Jim usually replies, "I didn't think to ask."

The Bible's anticlimactic announcement of Isaac's birth feels a bit like that: "They had the baby."

The truth is that when a moment in Scripture feels anticlimactic, it's probably because it is. The long awaited arrival— the one Abraham and Sarah thought would be the "Happily ever after" of their story—isn't the climax after all. The emotional pinnacle of this story comes a few chapters later, when the narrator slows the pace down, building up our anticipation with a startling word from God.

"God said, 'Take your son, your only son whom you love, Isaac, and go to the land of Moriah. Offer him up as an entirely burned offering there on one of the mountains that I will show you'" (Genesis 22:2).

Here's a story that never makes it into the children's Bibles. Who would ever want to read it as a bedtime story? It makes most of us extremely uncomfortable, the unimaginable demand God makes of Abraham. To require such heartbreak from any family would be unthinkable, but to ask this kind of sacrifice from a couple who waited so long for to hold the joy of the child in their arms? It's a scandalous thought.

This is the climactic question of Abraham and Sarah's story. Will they follow God's will, or will they continue to take control, playing God themselves?

At stake here is the family vocation—the calling to be a blessing to others. So far, Abraham and Sarah have failed miserably to even bless those within their own household (think Hagar and Ishmael). Now God wants to determine whether they have grown into their calling to bless the entire world.

With the arrival of their biggest dream come true, Isaac, their questions about God's reliability have been answered, but God has good reason to test their reliability, their faithfulness. With their heart's desire in their arms, who will hold center stage in their lives and decision making? Who will they bow down to? The altar of sacrifice will answer this question once and for all: When God gifts you with your heart's desire, will you worship the Giver, or will you worship the gift? To whom will you cling?

Perhaps even more surprising than God's difficult command is Abraham's immediate response. This time, without questioning, he obeys.

Abraham has been wandering and traveling for most of his story, but this journey up Mount Moriah with Isaac in tow has to be the longest journey of his life. There must have been a lot of time on that long walk to think about what he was going to do. And of course, there was Isaac right there behind him, making his way along the path in his father's careful footsteps, following with a child's trustful gait.

Abraham built an altar at the top. Then, taking Isaac is in his arms, he held the gift close for as long as he could stand, and offered him back to the Giver. *Not my will but yours be done.*

The image of Abraham standing over the altar with knife raised, poised to plunge it into his son Isaac's heart in obedience to God, is one that haunts me. It has popped into my head at the strangest moments. Holding my newborn baby his first night on earth. Standing before the church altar, bread raised, ready to offer the body in sacrifice again to the body of Christ. But, most unusually, presiding over the altar of another sacred moment the church: baptism.

For some reason, when I stand as a pastor in front of the church to participate in the baptism of a baby, when I take that squirming bundle dressed in white from his or her mother's arms, it's often this picture of Abraham and Isaac that appears in my mind. It has to do with sacrifice, and with the looks on the parents' faces in that holy and terrifying moment. For years, before I was a parent myself, I watched the mothers' expressions as they held out their squirmy bundles. Their mouths smiled, but the fear in their eyes communicated wordlessly: Please. Please don't squirm so hard that I almost drop you as I hand you to the pastor. Please don't scream and cry in front of the whole congregation. Please don't spit up on the pastor's stole or belch loudly into the microphone clipped to her robe. (I've had babies do all of these things at their baptisms!)

I've stood on the opposite side of the altar rail from parents so many times, trying my best to reassure those mothers with my calm smile. But inside I'm praying right along with them for the mercy of a calm baby. It's been one of the greatest privileges of my role as a pastor to receive those babies into my arms, representing both the arms of the church and the arms of God, and to speak those holy words over them: "I baptize you in the name of the Father and the Son and the Holy Spirit." To speak God's love over them and to seal their adoption into his family.

In the best of scenarios, the child sleeps through the whole thing, not even waking when a splash of cold water crosses their brow. Those are my favorite moments. Not just because all possible baptismal foibles have been averted, but because I see in my arms the perfect picture of how we all receive God's grace—so unaware of its depths that we mostly sleepwalk through it all.

It wasn't until the dark years of infertility and miscarriages that I realized how I longed to stand on the other side of the rail. The babies we lost never had a chance at baptism except in the waters of my womb. They were God's children nevertheless, sent the express route straight back to him, too early for us to name them or claim their place here in the church that I love. It was hard to hand the dream of those children back over to God.

When the day finally came that I could officially claim the title Mother, I realized that this was just practice for the ultimate vocation of parents—handing our children over to God. It's a lifetime process. Holding my newborn son, and then my daughter, I understood a little more the look in those mothers' eyes at the baptismal font, and their slight hesitation as they passed their treasures to me, dressed in slippery baptismal gowns. I understood the split-second desire to cling to our children, and the realization that it will recur again and again. In the act of handing them over, they were formally claiming the line that all parents who trust Christ must say: "This is not my child. This is God's child. I will use every last ounce of my energy and resources to care for this child. I will raise this child in faith, but ultimately this child is not mine. This child came from God and someday will return to him. This is God's child."

Before one of my children's baptisms, a good friend, who was also a pastor, asked if I'd be doing the baptism myself, if I'd dip my own hand into the water and wipe it on my baby's brow. I was surprised at the force of my response, my own gut reaction producing a loud and vocal, "No!" It wasn't that I didn't want to bless my child. It was just that I wanted to claim my only chance to stand on the opposite side of that altar rail. My closest friends in ministry could stand in the place of pastor for that day, but only I could stand in the mother's place, and I knew I needed to. I needed to place my babies into the arms of the church because I needed the reminder of what I had known long before they were born: "This is God's child."

I need the memories of that day, their pictures in white frames with crosses on my walls, to remind me of this fact every time I'm tempted to plan their lives out for them; every time I'm tempted to control them with my disapproval or direct their future with my worry; every time my priorities and decisions reveal that I worship them, giving an invisible God a backseat to the visible gifts I hold so dear. Every time I want so badly to be god in their lives, I need to remember that I officially gave up that job the day I handed them over to the arms of God and his church.

I have never had to face the decision Abraham faced. Thank God, most of us never will. But at some point in our lives, all of us will hold someone we love in our arms and in our hearts, and we will be faced with a question: Will you entrust this person to God? Will you be able to trust the Giver with the life of the gift?

Nearly every time I get to the end of Abraham's story, I exhale a sigh of relief. I'm sure my relief is nothing compared to Abraham's.

> But the Lord's messenger called out to Abraham from heaven, "Abraham? Abraham?" Abraham said, "I'm here." The messenger said, "Don't stretch out your hand against the young man, and don't do anything to him. I now know that you revere God and didn't hold back your son, your only son, from me." (Genesis 22:11-12)

Abraham didn't stop to ask why. Knife lowered, ropes untied, Abraham obeyed again. And exhaled. Just as Abraham had predicted when Isaac asked the hard question, "We have the wood, but where is the sacrifice?" God provided a lamb.

At his own Son's baptism, God couldn't resist the chance to show up as a proud parent. The Gospel of Mark declares that heaven was "torn open" as the Holy Spirit descended on Jesus like a dove. "You are my Son, whom I love; with you I am well pleased" (Mark 1:10-11 NIV).

The man doing the baptizing, Jesus' cousin John, declared that Jesus was "the Lamb of God who takes away the sin of the world" (John 1:29). That connection to the lamb, the one provided so that Isaac could be spared, was more than a coincidence. Jesus would echo the language used to describe Isaac when he reminded us in that iconic verse declaring him to be God's Son, his only Son. "God so loved the world that he gave his only Son, so that everyone who believes in him won't perish but will have eternal life" (John 3:16).

There are a lot of things I don't understand. I don't fully understand God's purpose in asking Abraham to place his son on the altar of sacrifice, or why he gave him an out at the last second. But one purpose is clear—the way this story sends shivers down our spine, picturing a father's love for his son who is about to be sacrificed, gives us just a tiny glimpse into just what a weighty and serious act of love for us it was for God to watch his Son die on a cross.

There are churches who don't baptize babies at all, who reserve the sacrament of baptism for adults, who can be dunked down into the water and raised up again just as Jesus was. There are Christians who faithfully read the Bible in different ways and come out with passionate and biblical arguments on both sides of that discussion, and we do well to respect one another's practices and biblical interpretations.

But one argument I can't ever quite get behind is this: the idea that we should reserve baptism for adults because it should be only for those who fully understand what they are doing in that moment. It causes me to wonder: Can any of us ever fully understand the amazing gift of Jesus Christ? Can you? Can I?

Probably not, but maybe the story of a father able to release his clinging grasp and lay his son on an altar to die helps us fathom just a bit more the depth of love God had for his people when he spared us, but not his own Son on the cross. Maybe Abraham's altar is there to help us to get it—as much as we ever can—to grasp how high and deep and wide God's love is for us. Maybe it is there to help us think in very human terms about how hard it is to hold our own children with open hands, lifting them as an offering, trusting them to God, our impulse so often to clutch them to our chests like possessions. The harder we try to keep them, the less we will succeed. In truth, they were never ours to begin with.

My own son, my only son, was baptized on Halloween, a date we scheduled for convenience sake, not giving any thought to the significance of the holiday. In retrospect, it seemed appropriate, though, to declare the powers of light would prevail in his life on a day when some choose to celebrate darkness.

That Halloween, I got to sit in the special front pew in the church for the first of only two times in my life: the pew reserved for the families of children being baptized. I got to stand in the spot I had longed to stand in for years, to stand opposite those who would take my child from my protective arms and claim him for God.

Just for the occasion, I had removed my clerical costume and come as myself. Just a mom. Holding a baby. Handing him over to God and his family. Whispering the words every parent must: this is God's child.

CHAPTER 6

Rebekah
Cascade

I LIKE TO TALK. JUST ASK MY HUSBAND, my closest friends, or my church. It's a good thing that God has called me to teach and preach, since it's the perfect arrangement: I get to talk—and a captive audience sits and listens!

That gift proved useless during a period, early in my ministry, when I was assigned an internship at a church called Christo Reina (Christ Reigns). If it's not obvious from the name, it was a church where everyone spoke fluent Spanish. Everyone, that is, but me. During my ministry there, my love for speaking was definitely not my greatest asset.

The church's leadership graciously decided that the area where I could be the most help (and probably do the least damage with my crude attempts to communicate) would be teaching an ESL class—English as a Second Language. Not only would I be helping first-generation Americans learn English, it would give me a chance to improve my Spanish. And trust me, it needed a lot of help.

Our class met each week at the home of one of the families in the church. Originally from Mexico City, both the husband and the wife were known for being wonderful cooks. This turned out to be a glorious gift. Each week, the hosts invited us to come an hour before class to partake of a huge, homemade authentic Mexican feast. I realized just how special this labor of love was when I found out that both the husband and wife were cooks in the kitchen of a local restaurant. They spent all day making food for strangers, and yet on Tuesdays rushed home to whip up a huge meal for our class. They really had the gift of making people feel welcomed and special.

Each week their delicious generosity deepened our friendship and helped me learn so much more than a few new vocabulary words in Spanish. A lot of what I learned was about hospitality, about going the extra mile to serve someone. The culture I was brought up in would say, "We'll order a pizza," or even, "Why don't you just grab something to eat before you come to class?" But the heart of hospitality this family exhibited was not just about doing the bare minimum, it was about going the extra mile to make sure their guests felt comfortable and welcome and very, very full. I noticed that I left their home each week well fed on food and friendship, and that the kindness I received there in that kitchen tended to cascade over to other people in my life. Generosity beget generosity. It was far more than I would have ever expected, and it was a blessing I'll never forget.

Our next encounter with the Genesis family reveals a

young woman who had that kind of gift, the gift of going above and beyond for others.

When we step back into their story, Sarah and Abraham's miracle baby Isaac is all grown up, but still a bachelor at age forty. This is a detail that apparently concerns Isaac's aging father, Abraham, who knows he's approaching his last days on earth and thus the last chance to marry off his boy. The weight of the decision about who Isaac will marry is even more significant, since she will play a part in fulfilling God's continuing promise that their family's descendants would eventually be as numerous as the stars.

Arranged marriage is a foreign concept to us in a culture that prizes individuality and the right to personal choice. Most people shudder to think of letting their parents make this huge life decision for them if arranged marriage was the norm today. Not only does Isaac not get to choose for himself, Abraham is too old to make the trip, so he sends his most trusted servant back to his hometown of Haran, five hundred miles away, to find Isaac a wife. Now imagine that it's not even your dad picking your spouse but your dad's closest friend or business associate!

Although the servant isn't given a name in this story, many people assume that it is Eliezer, Abraham's trusted servant and close friend. Abraham once lamented that since he didn't have a son or heir, his servant Eliezer would be the one who would become his heir, inheriting his property (Genesis 15:2). That simple fact illustrates just how close this relationship must have been, blurring lines between friendship and family.

Those who study families often talk about two stages of our family life: *family of origin* and *family of choice*. Our family of origin is the family that launches us, the family that lived in our house when we were growing up and gave us our start and our support system. Our family of choice, however, are people related by the ties of friendship rather than by blood, those with whom we share connections that are chosen rather than inherited. They are the friends who become like family to us. These are people we choose for ourselves as those we trust and count on as deeply as we do family itself.

I grew up in a small family of two, an only daughter raised by a single mom. Whenever I overheard someone whisper that I came from a "broken home," I felt confused. Nothing about my home seemed broken at all to me. Our house was a happy, contented place, filled with love and laughter. My mom did a million things right to bring me up in a way that formed me in God's image and filled me with his blessings. One of the greatest of those was raising me in the community of the church.

In our small, red-brick church, I felt at home, safe, and loved. My mom sang in the choir, so from about age four I sat "alone" in the congregation—only I was never alone. I sat with a different family each week, choosing my favorite adult seatmates based on how "soft" they were to fall asleep on as a pillow. God's previously mentioned sense of humor meant that after falling asleep in all of those church services as a child, I would grow up to become a preacher, trying to keep people awake in my own sermons.

Each of those families truly became family to us. We often referred to them as "back-door friends," meaning we could just walk in the back door of their house without even knocking. Instead of feeling deprived because I lived in a home inhabited by only two people, I knew that I had many families I could turn to for nurture, love, and support.

Family is not always a group of people related by blood. Often they are the people we rely on and turn to when we need a place of comfort and encouragement. Most of those families from our little hometown church are people we are still close with today. Now it brings me joy to see them ooh and aah over my children as if they were their own grandchildren. I'm so thankful that God sometimes gives us wonderful families by the circumstances of our birth but often adds to our kin by bringing people to walk beside us as a family we will have a chance to choose for ourselves.

Since Abraham was on his own (Sarah has already died) and too old to go search for a wife for Isaac, he chose a servant to do the job a family member usually did, someone he trusted like a brother. This was the most important errand the servant would ever undertake: go back to the family's original home, find Isaac a nice girl next door, and bring her back for him. This man must know Abraham and his values well enough to be able to choose as Abraham himself would choose.

If this trusted servant who is like family to Abraham is indeed Eliezer, who is mentioned in Genesis 15:2, he is well named. Eliezer means "God is help" or "Helper of God."

The first part of his name, el, is shorthand, referring to God: Elohim. The second half comes from the Hebrew verb ezer, which means to help or to support. It is the root of the same word given to Eve as a title the moment she was created. Eve's designation of "helpmate" was an indication that the main vocation of humans in relationship is to be a help one another. Eliezer, Helper of God, is a fitting name for a servant, and this servant in particular, since his heart matches his name.

This was probably the most important errand Abraham's servant would ever be sent on, and took it very seriously. He loaded ten camels with the supplies to make the five-hundred-mile trip. That three-week-long journey, moving at a camel's pace, gave him lots of time to think about what kind of woman he would look for as a wife for Isaac. It also gave him a lot of time to pray.

As he rode into the town where Abraham was from, the place he expected to find a wife for Isaac, he prayed this prayer:

God, when I stop and wait by this spring, I pray that the young woman who comes and not only offers me a drink of water, but offers water to all of my camels as well, would be the woman who is right for Isaac. Let her be the one.

This was a culture where hospitality was very important. If a stranger asked for a drink of water, it would be rude, even shameful for a young woman to refuse. But no one would expect her to water his camels too. That would've been above and beyond, up to 250 gallons for these twenty-five thirsty camels. So what he was praying for was an unusually generous young woman.

Instead of saying, "God, send Isaac a wife who is beautiful or brilliant or gifted or wealthy," the servant asked God to send Isaac a wife who had a heart to serve, who would go above and beyond for others, who would take what time and resources she had and enthusiastically give them away.

Someone who was blessed to be a blessing.

Sound familiar? That was the family motto, their calling—that they would take God's blessings and pour them generously out into the rest of the world. While it looked like this was a search for the right wife for Isaac, on a bigger scale, it was really about finding a woman who would help bring about God's greater plan.

Abraham's servant asked God to guide his selection of the young woman who would marry Isaac—and he asked for a beautiful, giving heart. God wasted no time in answering this prayer. While the servant was still praying, a young woman described as beautiful and pure showed up at the well.

I love the description of this event—that even before he finished praying, God has begun answering. We long for our prayers to be answered. We yearn to see God show up in our lives. But God also thrills to show off his love and power for his children. This was definitely one of those "show off" moments, because the young woman responded to his request for a drink exactly as he had prayed: "Let me get some water for your camels too."

With a two-gallon jar or pitcher, that offer might have taken her over three hours to fulfill. This was no easy task. Her kindness, her determination and desire to give above and beyond what was expected were Rebekah's greatest gifts. She had no idea how her service that day would change her life. She didn't know that her simple offer of kindness to a stranger would lead to a husband, a fortune, a legacy, a place in history, a place in eternity.

Rebekah had no idea what kind of results her kindness would bring that day. Instead of daydreaming or looking for a different future, her future found her while she was busy being faithful.

I've listened to single friends daydreaming out loud about the ideal man they would like to marry. As a matter of fact, I did a lot of daydreaming about the same thing when I was single. But Rebekah isn't spending her days preoccupied with looking for the right man. She is too occupied with being the right kind of woman. She is not daydreaming about Mr. Right. She is just being Miss Right with God.

My friend Charlotte was the one among our group of friends who always talked about wanting to get married and have children. When she met David, it seemed like God had answered her prayers. They had been dating for some time, and things were beginning to get serious, so they moved in together. To Charlotte, it seemed like an obvious step toward marriage, but nothing seemed obvious to David. He evaded the topic of matrimony as skillfully as if it were a professional sport.

Charlotte was beginning to feel that this might not be her "happily ever after" after all. She told me that she sent up prayer after prayer, asking to find God's will for her future marriage. When we talked about God's will, it was clear that she saw it as a future page on her life's script, the ultimate answer to the question, "How will things turn out?" It was harder to see God's will as part of the present—something that would influence her actions in her present relationship to honor God's wishes for her life.

I wasn't sure how to explain that God's will was not only about finding Mr. Right but also about being Miss Right. I searched for a way to gently explain that God's will is just as much about following his ways as it is finding his path. Like my friend Charlotte, many of us reach out to God for guidance on the subject of his will without taking him up on the lessons of his will that he has already made clear to us in his word.

I've also listened to married women complain about how they wish their husbands would be more like the ideal man they have pictured in their heads. You know him—the one who regularly gives flowers and compliments and offers to listen to you talk about your day while he cleans the bathrooms, puts the kids to bed, and makes a gourmet meal all at the same time. Too often in marriage, our focus is on getting the other person to meet our expectations, rather than fulfilling God's expectations for our own behavior. I have to tell myself weekly—it's always better for me to work on being the kind of person I'd like to be married to rather than working on changing my husband.

The same is true for all of our relationships. Rather than trying to get others to measure up to our expectations, berating them with our words, or trying to manipulate them with our disapproval, we would do well to focus on our own behaviors. After a lot of fruitless work, I've begun to realize that there's only one person I can change, and that's myself. All of our friendships and family relationships would probably improve if we followed Rebekah's example of showering others with kindness.

The results God had in mind must have come as a complete surprise to Rebekah. When she had finished her chore, this grungy, tired old stranger to whom she had shown kindness suddenly jumped up and began pulling out expensive jewelry! "When the camels had finished drinking, the man took out a gold nose ring weighing a beka and two gold bracelets weighing ten shekels" (Genesis 24:22 NIV).

This was a sign indicated that he was proposing marriage on behalf of a very rich and important man. The cultural differences between today's world and the way life was lived in biblical days fascinates me. I guess nothing says, "Will you marry my boss's son?" quite like a really nice nose ring!

Rebekah was swept up into the love story that followed. After she and her family agreed to the proposal, she traveled back with the servant to a new husband, a new land, and a new life—taking the same path of surrendering the familiar in favor of the promise that Abraham and Sarah once traveled. Although she and Isaac were strangers at the start, they grew to care deeply for one another. Their story features the Bible's first mention of romantic love.

Most romantic movies would wrap up their story here,

calling it "Happily Ever After," and being done with it. Julia Roberts as Rebekah and Tom Cruise as Isaac would ride off into the sunset (probably on a camel), and we'd watch the credits roll.

But if you want to get to the really juicy part of the story, you need to follow the happy couple after they get hitched. That's where things get interesting.

Add a couple of kids to the mix, and see how Julie Roberts looks at 3 a.m. when the toilet overflows, the baby has colic, and the dog starts throwing up on the couch. Better yet, give them twins and see how they handle that!

Rebekah and Isaac's twins were named Jacob and Esau. The womb may have been the only thing the two boys ever shared in common. They were as different as night and day, and so were their parents' feelings for them. "The boys grew up, and Esau became a skillful hunter, a man of the open country, while Jacob was content to stay at home among the tents. Isaac, who had a taste for wild game, loved Esau, but Rebekah loved Jacob" (Genesis 25:27-28 NIV).

Here is where Rebekah's story begins to sour.

Somehow the passage of time has turned Rebekah from a young woman who showed unimaginable generosity for a stranger to a mother who was tight fisted with the one resource her family needed the most. When it came to love, Rebekah traded her generosity for stinginess. As her twins grew up, Rebekah somehow got the idea that in order to give to one, she had to take away from the other. So she played favorites. So did Isaac.

Favoritism in a family comes out of the mistaken notion that love is a limited resource. Instead of believing they had more than enough love, more than enough attention, more than enough forgiveness and understanding, Rebekah's family was acting as if there was never enough. So each parent favored one child over the other—and the results were disastrous. Jacob and Esau developed jealousy and animosity that grew to a rivalry that would divide the entire family for years.

They didn't realize that love given could be love multiplied, not subtracted. We don't have to pick and choose where we give our love, as if it will run out if not guarded carefully. We can ask God to replenish our resources, giving us enough for the needs around us.

Sadly, these are the only two stories we really know from Rebekah's life. Her first big scene is one of generosity with her time and service as a young woman. Her last is tarnished with stinginess—a lack of ability to give love and blessing. It's this scene that ended up dividing a family.

In our modern households, having vastly different behavior on the inside of our homes than we have on the outside can be the result of something called Sunset Fatigue. We've all reached a point at one time or another when we come to the end of a long day, and "those who need our love the most, those to whom we are most committed, end up getting the leftovers. Sunset fatigue is when we are just too tired, or too drained, or too preoccupied, to love the people to whom we have made the deepest promises."[1]

I can relate. I often drive home at the end of a long day of meeting people's needs to find a long list of needs waiting there for me too. Should I walk in the door and announce that I'm off the clock? Done for the day? Or should I remind myself that I'm the only mom, the only wife, the only daughter that they get? You don't get to call in "tired" at home and be off the hook. In our families we are one of a kind, irreplaceable. That means working to find ways to bring them our best—not our leftovers.

My friend and mentor, Dr. Ellsworth Kalas, is known as one of the best preachers and authors in the church today. He's a grandfather now, but when his children were growing up, the church where he was a pastor was on the way home from his son's elementary school. Most days after school, his son would walk home and stop by to sit down in his dad's office, have a Coke and talk. Dr. Kalas would come around from his desk and sit down in a chair next to his son, talk about whatever was on the boy's mind, and then send him on his way home.

Years later, his son grew up to be a pastor himself. At some point, he began to realize what a huge workload his dad must've had each day as the senior pastor of that large church when he was a boy. He said to him, "You must've been so busy! You really made it seem like you had nothing better to do than to talk to me when I would stop by each day."

His dad's response was, "I didn't. I never had anything to do that was more important than spending time with you."

Abundance and generosity need to start in our own homes: in the relationships closest to us. We need to orient our lives in ways that say this is the most important place to be generous with our time, our attention, our patience, our praise, and our forgiveness. We're not talking about giving to the point of exhausting ourselves, not having enough time and energy to take care of ourselves. That's getting back to the mentality of scarcity, where we give so much that there's not enough left over for us. It's the idea of living life abundantly that we're after.

Jesus said, "I came so that they could have life—indeed, so that they could live life to the fullest" (John 10:10).

The God who has more than enough for us gives abundantly, so our blessings can cascade to others. God replenishes our generous hearts with his own abundance and generosity.

The reason for Rebekah's favoritism of Jacob is vague. Maybe it was just to balance things out since his twin, Esau, was the clear favorite of their dad. But Isaac's preference for Esau is given with a very clear explanation.

Esau was a hunter who brought home meat, and Isaac had a taste for wild game. Some wild boar bacon, a little venison sausage, these were the ways to Isaac's heart. Isaac's love for his son was based on the father's appetites, not the son's attributes. He favored Esau because his son gave him something he wanted and hungered for. That's a pretty selfish definition of love.

Isaac and Rebekah's family story makes me feel sad. Sad for them. Sad for their children and the legacy that comes from the mentality of scarcity. It also makes me feel scared. Anxious that I'll fall into the same trap that they did, choos-

ing to dole out love as a reward. Nervous that my relationships will be marred by love with strings attached. I don't
want to choose who or how I love because someone feeds my
appetites in some way.

My daughter is a toddler now, and her daily discoveries of
the simplest things give me such joy. But there is one concept
she has not yet learned that brings frustration on an almost
daily basis. It's the concept of *if/then*. If you eat one more
bite, then I'll let you get down from your highchair. If you'll
just stop crying, then I can figure out what you're asking for.
If you finish your dinner, then you can have the candy you've
been pointing at on top of the fridge.

The problem is that the words *if* and *then* just don't have
any meaning in her vocabulary yet. If she sees candy, she wants
to eat it. Now. If she wants something, I should get it for her.
For Kate at twenty months old, life is not yet conditional. This
deficiency in vocabulary makes for some very noisy sessions at
our dinner table. I'm so ready for her to get it.

On the other hand, I'm not sure I want Kate to understand that the world is conditional. Right now she believes
that love flows her way no matter what she does, how she
acts, how loudly she screams. We have poured love into her
from her first moments here on earth and she has learned
the lesson well: our love is not stopped by noisy behavior. It
knows no conditions.

While I look forward to being able to communicate a little
better about our rules around the dinner table, I don't want

Kate to learn that feeding my appetites is a condition for approval or love. I don't want to offer my children approval just because they make the grades I wish they would, or excel in the activities that are important to me, or behave in public in a way that makes me look good. I don't want to reserve my friendship for people who feed my appetite to look important or to be told only what I want to hear. I want to give to those I love abundantly for who they are, not withhold my love until they act the way my appetites demand.

In his book, *The Blessing*, John Trent tells a story about his own mother, who raised him and his two brothers by herself as a single mother. It wasn't easy, he says, but she poured every ounce of love she had into her three boys.

Later in life, when they would visit her in her condo, there was one piece of furniture in her house that held deep meaning for her boys. To a stranger's eye it might have gone unnoticed, but to the family it symbolized the kind of love and affection this woman lavished on her children. It was a simple bookshelf. There was nothing extraordinary about its shape or design—it was the books it contained that were so curious. One shelf was filled with theology and psychology books. Another had textbooks about the practice of medicine and the study of genetics. Trent says, "The third shelf seemed most out of place for a seventy-six-year-old, arthritic woman. Lining that shelf were dozens of issues of Heavy Equipment Digest and how-to books on driving heavy equipment."[2]

This strange reading material made much more sense if you knew her sons—and especially if you knew her unqualified love for them. John, the son who wrote about her story, has authored several books on theology and psychology. His twin brother, Jeff, is an oncologist who specializes in genetic research. And the construction equipment? Their older brother Joe is a heavy-equipment operator, a fact she took as much pride in and told friends about as excitedly as she did about her son the author and her son the doctor. She loved them each for who they were, not for who she wanted them to be—and she showed her love and blessing by learning all she could about their work so she could appreciate their gifts.

When their mother passed away and her three boys went to clean out her home, that difficult task that many people face when they lose a parent—when they went and looked over all the things she owned, things she cared about—it was the bookshelf that they wept over the most.

Sometimes we choose to give love or approval to our children or our family members or friends or others in our lives based on who we want them to be, not on who they are. But unconditional love, the kind of love God has for us, isn't based on anything we can offer to God—it's based on the simple fact that we are his children. I want to be sure that I'm loving my children, my family, my friends based on who they are—not on who I want them to be. I want to love them unconditionally, just as God loves me. I want the cascade of generosity to begin in my own home and flow out from there, whether in lavish meals or hugs or the patience and forgiveness we all need on a frequent basis. I want for those who cross my path to feel that love does not run out, that there's always more than enough to go around.

CHAPTER 7

Jacob and Esau
Competition

I WAS AN ONLY CHILD GROWING UP, but I was never lonely or bored. I was the kind of kid easily entertained with the world between the pages of a good book or simply being left alone with my own vivid imagination. Part of my imaginary world did include wondering what it would be like to have a brother or sister. In my mind, it seemed almost magical to have a built-in playmate and partner in crime—a brother who would watch over and protect me or a sister who would giggle with me and braid my hair.

Strangely enough, my friends weren't living out this fairy tale of sibling bliss that I had conjured up in my imagination. When I visited their homes, I saw relationships between brothers and sisters that seemed less like an episode of *Little House on the Prairie* and more like *Lord of the Flies*. Because I had no personal experience with siblings, I was always a little confounded by the jealousy and hostility that arose in this most personal of family relationships.

Had I read Genesis, I might have understood. Genesis is especially candid about the bittersweet relationship between the earliest of peers, siblings. From beginning to end, it spins tales of sibling rivalry that are at once horrific and completely believable. As the first siblings, Cain and Abel set the stage for the Bible's legacy of "brotherly love" with the first episode of fratricide. The brothers Jacob and Esau wrestle in the womb and then throughout their lives for dominance and possession of power and inheritance. Sisters Rachel and Leah compete for a husband's love and use their children as collateral in a lifelong rivalry. Even in the last major generation of Genesis, Joseph and his brothers are still fighting, bragging, contemplating murder, selling a brother into slavery, and picking up the pieces of their family years down the road.

If we ever needed assurance that it's perfectly normal for brothers and sisters to experience strong feelings of both love and hatred toward one another, Genesis offers us proof! But however natural our bent towards competition with our closest companions may be, we need to keep those feelings closely in check. What we learn in our earliest days has the tendency to creep out into other relationships, not just among brothers but with colleagues, friends, enemies. And feelings of competition can be the drop of poison in the well of relationships that spreads silently and quickly, with deadly consequences.

Jacob and Esau present one of the most colorful biblical accounts of a sibling pair. Their early life (starting in utero) is filled with conflict and strife. My husband, with his wry humor, would call Jacob and Esau "womb mates." They are twins, and even though we might expect that to engender certain similarities, they are different in every way.

How can two people who come from the same mix of DNA, share the same womb, and grow up in the same household be so different? That's a question that parents are still scratching their heads over today.

Even Jacob and Esau's names mark them as opposites from the beginning. Esau's name is simple, given without hidden meaning or nuance. He is born covered in red hair (an unusual sight for a baby, for sure!), so his parents name him "Hairy" (*Esau* in Hebrew.) The midwife delivering him had not even gotten the words, "It's a boy!" out of her mouth when she noticed that right on his heels—literally grabbing onto Esau's heel with his chubby little hand—was his younger brother, younger by the slimmest margin of time possible. Jacob emerges into the world grasping at his brother as if to say, "Oh no you don't! I wanted to be first." His name is symbolic, action driven, laced with a subversive meaning. *Jacob* means "Grabby." But it also means deceiver, supplanter, one who grabs hold of what is not his and takes it for his own.

Hairy and Grabby. Not the most creative choices, but descriptive, you have to admit. Jacob will grow up to live into the meaning behind his name. You never know, with Jacob, when his words are laced with deception and self-interest. Like his name, his actions are always full of double meanings. Esau, on the other hand, grows up to be a face value kind of guy. With him, you always know what you are getting. He is ruddy, hairy, outdoorsy, and loves to hunt and provide. He will be plain with his needs, his sorrow, his anger. Esau is just as easy to read as Jacob is difficult to decipher.

Jacob's interest in grabbing hold of his firstborn brother is more than just a matter of neonatal rivalry. Those few seconds by which he missed the firstborn title meant that Jacob would grow up always comparing his lot in life to his brother—who was now set to inherit both the family birthright and blessing.

Jacob was born in a day when the perennial sibling battle cry of "It's not fair!" was more than a battle over later bedtimes or number of Christmas presents. The birthright means that the oldest son, the one who happens to be born first, will collect a disproportionately large share of the inheritance and eventually take his father's place as family patriarch. His position as firstborn would, upon the death of his father, make him ruler of the family, including his siblings, a fact recognized from birth. The birthright meant that if Jacob was ever tempted to whine at his older brother (as younger siblings are prone to do), "You're not the boss of me!" he would be wrong.

The birth of twins must have made it even clearer how arbitrary this practice was. The older twin wasn't necessarily stronger or smarter or more equipped to lead; he was simply first, even if by only a few seconds. That injustice troubled Jacob from childhood. What was so special about Esau that he should inherit the entire estate and rule the family? Jacob glared miserably at the "greener grass" on Esau's side of the fence. He fumed and plotted and waited for his chance.

His opportunity finally came when Esau returned from

a long hunting trip empty-handed and exhausted. Dragging himself into the kitchen, Esau declared, "I'm starving to death; what's there to eat around here?" And it just so happened that Jacob, little Grabby, had been cooking something up in more ways than one.

Jacob was eating the last bowl of prepared food in the house, a red stew. Even if there are more ingredients to prepare another batch, this is not the era of fast food. It's a time in which the recipe for chicken nuggets began with the phrase, "Go out back and kill a chicken." While Esau wasn't going to wait, Jacob was ready and waiting to take advantage of his brother's moment of weakness. He had been stewing to get what belonged to his brother since the moment of their birth, so he introduced the deal that would change both of their lives forever: Esau's birthright for one bowl of stew. Esau agrees and the deal is sealed.

Both brothers ended up with what they wanted, but neither was truly satisfied. Esau's bowl would satisfy for only a time, and he would be hungry again, this time without an inheritance to trade. Jacob's newly acquired birthright was just the beginning of an underhanded series of events that would cause so much devastation in the family that he would have to run away, making it impossible for him to enjoy the land, inheritance, and leadership he had seized. Grabbing for the things that look so good on someone else's plate never brings happiness in the end.

Unsatisfied with the birthright, Jacob bided his time until their father was close to death. And this time, he made his move to grab his brother's blessing as well. The spiritual blessing was far more than a "God bless you"—they understood it to be passing on the blessing that God had offered their family beginning with Abraham.

The stamp that meant the "blessed to be a blessing" was his to inherit. And Jacob's mother, Rebekah, Isaac's wife, who had always played favorites, helped him disguise himself as his older brother, sneak into the room where his now-blind father lay dying, and convince him that he was Esau instead—tricking him so that he could grab away the blessing that rightfully belonged to his brother.

Since they weren't that many generations removed from the very first brothers—Cain and Abel—it suddenly became very important that Jacob change locations very quickly. That first story of sibling rivalry hadn't ended well. I believe a large percentage of time spent parenting siblings is about keeping the Cain and Abel story from happening all over again! Remember my earlier story about Jim and his sister, Ann, visiting their grandparents separately?

Knowing how enraged Esau would be when he discovered his brother's trickery, Jacob's mother packed him up and sent him off to stay with her brother and his family in a distant country. He was gone for decades, separated from his family, and though the land was now legally his, he couldn't even inhabit it for fear of the brother he had stolen it from. By competing to steal away his brother's rights, he ended up separating himself from the inheritance he had stolen and the family who loved him.

This desire that we see wrapped up in this family—the urge to compete with each other—may begin between brothers and sisters when we're small, but it doesn't stay there.

I had dinner a while back with friends who have two boys—one four and one not even two yet. I said, "I guess they're too young for you to have to deal with sibling rivalry, right?" She turned to the four-year-old and said, "Show Rev. Jessica your bite marks!"

Unfortunately, the family has sometimes served as a training ground for the urge we all struggle with: the human tendency toward competition with one another. Especially in cases like Jacob and Esau's family, where a parent plays favorites—and in their family both the mother and the father had a favorite, which didn't make things equal—it makes the competition even worse.

Sometimes our families feel like there just aren't enough resources to go around—maybe there's not enough time or attention for everyone to get what they need, or maybe it feels like there's just not enough love, so one parent might run out before we all get enough. That's definitely what it felt like in this family once Isaac gave a blessing to Jacob. When Esau showed up later, he asked, "Where's my blessing, Father, don't you have enough left for me?" His father basically didn't have a second blessing. Feeling like emotional resources in the family are scarce makes us want to compete with each other for the little that's there, and that competition becomes a habit.

Competition is often so deep-seated in us that we don't

even notice that we're doing it. But it can wound our souls and damage our relationships with others. Consider Jacob's story: he spent his entire childhood and early adulthood obsessed with what his brother had—it always seemed better to him—and he dreamed and schemed of ways he could take it away from him, defying God and almost irreparably damaging any relationship he could have with his own twin, Esau.

Esau isn't exactly faultless here. Genesis tells us he made the trade in the first place because he despised his birthright (Genesis 25:34). Jacob could not have taken what Esau was not willing to trade. Esau despised the future that he had been handed; he didn't want what had been passed down to him. While Jacob was wishing he was Esau, Esau was wishing that he was someone else.

We were each born with a kind of birthright, the details that make us uniquely who we are. But if we spend all our time measuring our birthright—our self—against someone else's, we're basically saying, like Esau, that we would trade our birthright, give our own gifts away, all for the want of what we see in someone else's hand.

When God begins to nudge me that he has a job for me—someone to love, someone to help, someone to confront or comfort—I often begin with an escape clause. I've sometimes answered God's call by telling him he has the wrong number. Sometimes I'm specific in letting God know who else might be better for this particular job than I am: *I'm sorry, God. I can't answer your call on my life. I can't go in the direction you're leading me or do the thing that you want me to do...because I happen to know I'm just not qualified for the job.*

I'm sorry God, but you must have the wrong house. If you'll just go two doors down you'll find a woman who is a much better housekeeper, who is more able to balance work and family, who sings like an angel and cooks like a chef. Someone who reads her Bible and prays for two hours each morning and night, who always has time for her friends and her husband and exercises eight times a week while she multitasks by writing out thank-you notes for the thank-you notes people have sent her.

You can't want me, God, because she's available. And really there's just no competition.

Setting ourselves up for perpetual comparison to others is like trading in our birthrights. When we do fall into the comparison trap, we tend to run away from what God has made us to be because he didn't create us like someone else.

When Genesis says Esau *despised* his birthright (Genesis 25:34 NIV), doesn't that mean, in a way, that he despised the One who gave it to him? That he questioned the goodness of the God of all good and perfect gifts?

If we want to live into our full potential as splendid creatures of a boundless creator, we need to stop giving away our birthright because they look better on someone else. Here's the truth: God has crafted you as his *masterpiece*. You are fearfully and wonderfully made. There are things God made in you that he made in no one else. There are things you are called to do for his kingdom that only you can fulfill.

Spending your time wishing you were something you are not says you don't trust that God did a good job when he made you—and that's just not possible. God doesn't make cheap goods, discounted merchandise, or mistakes.

While the birthright was given (appropriately) at birth, the gift of the blessing had to wait until there was a death in the family, specifically the death of the father.

God invented blessing. It was part of his original job description. When God forms, fills and lights the world, one thing he fills it with again and again is blessing. He is so eager to bless that when he created humans, it was the very first thing he did for them. "God created humanity in God's own image, in the divine image God created them, male and female God created them. God blessed them" (Genesis 1:27-28).

Humans have found ways throughout history to share this job description, to confer blessing on each other. In Jacob and Esau's generation, one of the primary ways of extending blessing was to bestow it on the patriarch of each generation. When the old family patriarch was about to die, he would call his oldest son in to give him the blessing that had been handed down for posterity. This blessing was so much more than a casual "God bless you" when someone sneezes. It was a serious spiritual commodity passed from father to son, the way that God's presence with the family continued to reside from one generation to the next.

The problem is that this communicated that there was only one blessing, for only one person, and it could be transferred on only one special occasion.

When grabby Jacob snuck into his dying father's room disguised as his older brother and stole the one available blessing, there wasn't another. Keeping with this family's practice of scarcity, there wasn't enough to go around for everyone. These brothers that had competed all their lives for what they could get from their parents were pushed into a position of all or nothing. You either got the blessing or you got none.

When Esau discovered that he had been swindled again, he was crushed. "Esau said to his father, 'Do you really have only one blessing, Father? Bless me too, my father!' And Esau wept loudly" (Genesis 27:38).

The sad thing about the way this culture interpreted blessing is how far the results were from God's original intent. Blessings are not a limited resource. They are far from scarce. But so many of us go through life assuming God exercises blessing in a limited way. When we witness the good in someone else's life, we begin to wonder why there isn't a blessing like that for us.

God always has more than enough blessing to go around. If we're busy checking out the good in other people's lives with an envious eye, we won't see the blessings God is pouring out on us.

God doesn't desire for us to bless only one person, or to reserve our kindness and generosity for special occasions. If we are to be like him, then we'll look for every chance to bless, every chance to love, every chance to let others know how special they are to us.

I was amazed by the story of a father who, like Isaac,

realized that he was approaching his last days on earth. When time is short, we often realize the urgency of the most important things we want to do in life, and this man decided to act to share blessing with those he loved the most before the chance disappeared.

Fred Evans had four children—three of them daughters. Like many fathers of daughters, he dreamed of walking his little girls down the aisle one day—and since one of them had married, he was still dreaming of taking that walk with the other two. But at age sixty-two, as Mr. Evans was recovering from a double lung transplant, he was diagnosed with melanoma. The medications from his transplant meant that he would be unable to undergo cancer treatment. Unable to do anything more for him, his doctors gave him just months to live.

Not one to give up on a dream, Mr. Evans came up with a plan. He decided to walk his other two daughters down the aisle and give them his blessing. And he decided he wouldn't wait for a wedding to do that. With the help of his wife and oldest daughter, he reserved a church, rented a tux, and waited for each of his younger daughters to arrive.

When the girls walked into the church, not knowing what was going on, they were escorted one at a time to the bride's room where their father was waiting. As they listened through tears he told them how loved they were, what a blessing they had been in his life. They heard again how he had always dreamed of walking them down the aisle since they were little girls. And then he did.

From the back of the sanctuary, they saw that their family and friends had gathered at the front of the beautiful church. Everyone stood as the organ played the bridal march, and then their father's dream was fulfilled. When he was done, he went back and did the same for his second daughter, and then announced that he had one more bride to walk down the aisle. To his wife's surprise he pulled her to the back of the sanctuary, walked her down the aisle as well, and renewed their vows at the front of the church.[1]

Very soon after that special day, Fred Evans lost his battle with cancer, but he had no unfinished business. He wanted to give his daughters his blessing, so he asked himself, *Why wait? Why wait for a special occasion? Why wait for there to be the right time or the right day? Today is the right time, it's the right day.*

God doesn't wait to give us his blessings. He pours them out freely, abundantly, daily—no special occasion needed. God wants to bless you! You don't have to trick him by pretending to be something you're not. You don't have to beg for his love. His blessings are yours for the taking. You don't have to compete against those closest to you for marks of status or success that will elude and disappoint. You only have to open your eyes, see the blessings that await each of us, and receive.

CHAPTER 8

Rachel and Leah
Comparison

IN HIGH SCHOOL, SHELLY AND AMBER were best friends. They sat together in every class at school and went home and talked on the phone all night. They spent most weekends at one or the other's house. But when they weren't together, it seemed they were always complaining to their parents that the other one had it better. Amber was an only child, and Shelly had three younger siblings, so Shelly was always telling her parents, "It's not fair! Amber never has to babysit!" Amber would tell her parents, "It's not fair! I have to do all the chores, and Shelly has brothers and sisters to help her do them." Shelly would say, "Amber gets more new clothes than I do." Amber would say, "Shelly gets to stay out later than I do."

It went back and forth like that until finally, both sets of parents were tired of it. So they got together and decided to teach their daughters a lesson. Long before reality TV was invented, they devised a way to give both girls a dose of reality, a scheme that could've been called "Daughter Swap." For a whole month, each girl had to live at the other one's house, do her chores, wear her clothes, and obey the other girl's parents as if they were her own.

When Shelly and Amber first heard about the plan, they thought it was going to be a great deal. But not even a week into their month of trading places, the parents started hearing that phrase again: "It's not fair!" It's not fair: I never have to do so many chores at home. My parents would never make me ride the bus to school. I never had to go to bed so early at home. It turned out that life in the other household held struggles and responsibilities all its own.

The girls were both grateful to return home at the end of the month. I don't think there was much complaining and comparing between the two after their little experiment was over.

Jacob and Esau led lives complicated by a rivalry of competition, but Jacob's two wives Rachel and Leah had an even greater struggle with the twin demon of comparison. Those two C words can wreak havoc in relationships and families. Competition and comparison pit us against those who are supposed to be supporters and allies, making us instead into rivals or even enemies.

Women can practice the art of comparison with pronounced skill and particular venom. Anyone who has attempted to become part of a community or collection of women will notice the gaze with which we are practiced at giving, sizing one another up to find our place in the invisible lineup only other women can see.

If "comparison is the thief of joy," as Theodore Roosevelt observed, then many of us have experienced the joy stolen right from under our noses as we gazed longingly at the grass on the neighbor's side of the fence.

Jacob's need for escape from the mess of his own making back at home, with an ailing father, scheming mother, and irate brother, pushed him to leave home and family as quickly as possible. He set off on the road to Harran, on a pathway well-worn by his family: Abraham and Sarah left Harran for the promised land of Canaan (Genesis 12:4-5) but sent a servant back to find Isaac's wife (and ultimately Jacob and Esau's mother), Rebekah.

Now Jacob heads to his mother's home with a similar errand in mind—to find a wife. Although our culture deems the marriage of close relatives taboo, in their culture a match made between cousins was considered a favorable one. The closest and most trusted ties were between family members within a clan or tribe. Why marry the girl next door if you don't even have to look outside the family compound?

When he gets to the home of his mother's brother, Laban, he finds there not one, but two unmarried and eligible cousins. Jackpot! "Now Laban had two daughters: the older was named Leah and the younger Rachel. Leah had delicate eyes, but Rachel had a beautiful figure and was good-looking" (Genesis 29:16-17).

The way the sisters are described sets up the comparison between them right away. Leah is described only as having "weak" eyes—but before we start feeling sorry for her, the description could mean that they are "soft" or "tender." But still, in contrast with the top billing her sister gets (Rachel has a gorgeous face and a great bod!), Leah's "nice eyes" are little consolation. That's almost as bad as being introduced as the sister who has a "nice personality." To add insult to insult, Rachel's name means "ewe lamb," a tender picture of a young female sheep—and perhaps a nod to her occupation as shepherdess—while the name Leah can also mean either "weary" or "cow."[1]

I'm sure these sisters grew up hearing people compare their looks and their names. The strain between them is apparent, as even the Bible casts them as rivals from the beginning. How can they not spend their lives obsessed with comparison? And what a setup for a dramatic rivalry when an eligible young cousin moves into their home looking for a wife.

Jacob quickly fell head over heels for Rachel, the younger sister. Certain that she was the girl for him, he struck a deal with her father, his uncle Laban, that he would work seven years in payment for marrying the most desirable of his two daughters.

What he didn't realize quite yet was that the deceptive nature that plagued him ran deep in his mother's side of the family. Jacob took Laban at his word that when those seven years ended, his marriage to Rachel would be his quick compensation, a mistake he would later regret. Even the crafty Jacob could be blinded by love, so he let his guard down. "Jacob worked for Rachel for seven years, but it seemed like a few days because he loved her" (Genesis 29:20).

This is one of the most romantic lines in the Bible. Even seven years of labor seems like a single day, since he's working for the one he loves. Jacob, the romantic. But his very next line reveals a different emotion—expressed directly to his intended's father: "The time has come. Give me my wife so that I may sleep with her" (Genesis 29:21).

Ah, men.

So Laban threw a great wedding banquet, a huge feast where all the friends and neighbors came together and ate and drank and were merry, and the groom ate and drank and was one of the merriest of them all. And at the end of the night, he stumbled into the very dark marriage tent with his very veiled bride and didn't realize until the morning that he had been duped.

There are plenty of jokes about a man marrying a woman who turns out not to be not the person he thought she was—but in this case it's actually true. Laban deceived Jacob and snuck his older and less desirable daughter Leah into the tent. Jacob went to sleep thinking he had married the lamb and awoke next to the cow! "When morning came, there was Leah! So Jacob said to Laban, 'What is this you have done to me? I served you for Rachel, didn't I? Why have you deceived me?'" (Genesis 29:25 NIV).

I love this part, because remember what Jacob's name means? Deceiver. Jacob literally shouted, "Why have you *Jacobed* me?" In a moment of clear comeuppance, someone has out-Jacobed the Jacob.

I wonder if Jacob realized the irony of what he was saying

the moment the words came out of his mouth. By condemning Laban's devious act, he was pointing a finger at himself. In the darkness of the marriage tent, Laban made a deceptive switch that would affect Jacob's life forever, giving the husband meant for the youngest daughter to the oldest. Jacob had deceived his own father, in the dark because of his failing eyesight, stealing the blessing meant for the oldest and turning tail to run.

It turns out you can't outrun your sins. They follow and show up in the strangest of places, begging for recognition until they are named.

While I would love to revel as Jacob meets his just reward, something about his story sparks an uncomfortable sense of recognition. I've been confronted with my own shortcomings in someone else's flaws more times than I'd like to admit. It usually happens like this: I meet someone who somehow rubs me the wrong way, and when I finally put my finger on what this person does that bugs me, I realize that it's one of my flaws too.

Early in our marriage, my husband and I went on a long car trip to visit some old friends. During the visit, I was annoyed again and again by the negative behavior of someone I had known for years. No matter who we talked about, they continued to point out things that were wrong with him or her. Toward the end of the visit, I was in a huff, tired of listening to my friend bad-mouthing person after person that we knew in common. By the time we got in the car to go home, I was ready to explode with pent-up frustration. I let

Jim have it with both barrels from the passenger's seat all the way home: how this person was incredibly negative, how they were bad-mouthing people they pretended to be friends with, how it ruined my visit to listen to the rehearsal of people's flaws nonstop. My sweet husband just drove and listened quietly. Too quietly. As if he heard something I had not yet recognized. By the time we were almost home, his silence gave me a chance to reflect on how guilty I was of complaining nonstop about someone who complained nonstop.

When we have a flaw in our character that we're unaware of, God sometimes holds up another person as a mirror to show us just what needs to change. That is especially true in our families, since resemblance rarely ends with our looks. Jacob found that he couldn't complain too long about Laban Jacobing him without seeing the ridiculous parallel to his own deceitful ways. The trap had been set, and Jacob was stuck with the wrong woman and an uncomfortable new self-awareness.

In the culture of the day, there was a bit of a different solution than divorce for mistakes in marital choice. Feel like you've married the wrong woman? No problem—just marry the right one too!

Jacob played "Let's Make a Deal" with Uncle Laban one more time. He finished the wedding feast for his marriage to Leah, and immediately began another, where he married the girl he had chosen in the first place, Rachel. The arrangement included working seven more years for the privilege of marrying both of Laban's daughters.

Now here's a recipe for disaster. Two sisters, already rivals from childhood, married to the same man. It's very clear that Jacob was solely in love with Rachel and had just sort of taken Leah along as part of the package, the way you take the side of broccoli on your plate beside your nice, wonderful, juicy steak. What Jacob was after was the main course, not the side dish.

Just as the favoritism displayed by Jacob and Esau's parents stirred up a terrible jealousy and conflict between them, Jacob's own preference of one wife over the other began a saga that would damage their family almost beyond repair.

Each of the two sister-brides felt lost and forgotten. When they looked at their sister's life, they saw the one thing they longed for most and couldn't have. What each sister wanted most of all was always just out of her reach. For Leah, it was her husband's love. For Rachel, it was the children she longed to bear, while Leah, Miss "Nice Personality," had several sons right away. Hatred brewed between the sisters. Suddenly their history of childish comparison became a very grown-up situation.

My friend Megan remembers a childhood filled with the joy of magical Christmases. The anticipation of seeing all the presents build up under the tree was almost more than she and her brother, Chris, could handle. For weeks leading up to the big day, they would crawl around checking the labels and shaking the ones that belonged to them to see if they could guess the contents.

On Christmas morning, Megan's excitement in opening

her own gifts was sometimes diminished when she looked over at her brother opening his. She remembers thinking to herself, *Chris got a lot of gifts. Did he get more than me? Did they spend more money on him this year? Do they love him more?* The atmosphere of comparison wasn't something that started with Megan. Their mom fixated on fairness, always being extremely careful to point out that neither child was given a treat, gift, or surprise unless the other child could have one too. Instead of making the brother and sister feel equally cared for, though, the emphasis on fairness only heightened the attention to their sibling's belongings and the expectation that they would always be treated the same. While Megan was a star student, the model of good behavior at school, Chris got into trouble a lot and needed extra attention and discipline, which made Megan feel like she was left in the shadows sometimes.

Megan's mom sometimes felt guilty about working outside the home, which complicated things further. When she gave her children gifts, she reminded them that the family could only afford nice things because she worked, so material possessions sometimes felt like a sign of their mother's love. Megan's habit of comparing her gifts to her brother's led to deeper questions about who was more valued.

Soon after Megan and Chris graduated from college, their parents announced the exciting news that each of the kids would be receiving a major gift: a new car. Megan remembers that her mom sat them both down on the morning of their car-buying trip and laid down a few rules. The first rule was that whereas Megan's car was a gift, free and clear, Chris would have to pay back a portion of his since his parents had helped him through a few financial scrapes in his college years. The purchase of the cars was one way of evening out the loans that had been made when Chris needed help, reinforcing the family's practice of stressing fairness.

Another rule was that these new cars were to be basic models, no luxury items included. As Megan's mom put it, "No chrome, no bells and whistles, and no sunroof." Megan and their father would shop for her car, while Chris and their mother would shop together and return to the house that afternoon to celebrate their purchases.

Later that afternoon, Megan stood in the driveway with her dad looking over her first brand-new car, feeling both pride and gratitude for her parents' generosity. But when Chris and their mom drove up, her heart sank. Chris's new car sported chrome wheels, a high-end sound system, and...a sunroof.

Megan found herself feeling like that little girl on Christmas morning all over again, equating larger gifts with greater love and feeling as if she had gotten the short end of both. Her mom, seeing Megan's crestfallen look, immediately apologized and explained what a great deal they had been offered for Chris's car. When that didn't soften Megan's disappointment, her mother drove her back to the dealership and traded up so that Megan could have a model of equal value.

Over the next few years, Megan thought a lot about her family relationships and about what made her feel loved and valued. The more she thought about it, the more she realized that the jealousy she experienced there could never make things right in the end. She resolved not to compare the gifts her parents offered, even when her resolve was challenged as it became clear they weren't going to make Chris pay them back for any portion of his car. Megan says, "I came to realize that you don't have to treat us the same in order to treat us equally." Her newfound perspective replaced the tension of constant comparison and gave her a sense of freedom and joy when she was with her family.

Rachel and Leah didn't reflect on and resolve their feelings the way Megan did. Instead they carried their petty childhood comparisons into adulthood and marriage. Who could win their husband's love? Who would have the offspring that confirmed her place as the matriarch of this future family? Rachel may have been the best loved by their husband, but her childlessness caused her great pain and grief. After Leah had several sons right away, Rachel worried that her sister was pulling ahead, so she came up with a plan. She offered her maid, Bilhah, to her husband as a concubine and surrogate mother for the children who would be considered Rachel's in this lifelong competition. Sound familiar? The plan was neither original nor ingenious. I wonder if Rachel realized how much heartache it had already caused for Jacob's grandmother, Sarah, or how much grief it could cause her own family.

When Rachel's maid began having sons, Leah responded by bringing in a pinch hitter of her own, creating the same arrangement with her own maid. Now there were four women in the same household sleeping with the same man, all using their offspring to keep score as the strange familial love triangle became a multisided polygon.

The race to have the most babies reminds me of the Toronto Stork Derby of 1936. That was the year that eccentric, wealthy Charles Millar died without an heir. Always one to appreciate a good wager, Millar left a provision in his will for the bulk of his inheritance to go to the woman who gave birth to the most babies in Toronto in the next ten years. As the Great Depression hit its stride, the allure of that fortune created a citywide frenzy among women, who began competing to see who could be the most prolific reproducer of the decade. Newspapers began following the stories of a handful of women who were neck-in-neck for the prize, creating mini-celebrities out of these growing families.

In the end, four women tied. Each of them gave birth to nine babies in ten years, and they split the inheritance, which gave them each $125,000, which I'm sure they spent immediately on diapers. All joking aside, I can't quite imagine life inside those households in a day when surely the life span of need far outlasted the fortune they received. Not to mention how it must have felt for the runners-up.

It's strange to think of women using their children as a tool for competition, unless you think about the competitions that surround our progeny today: "What colleges did *she* get into?" "How many points did *he* score?" "You mean she hasn't started crawling *yet*?"

Have you ever noticed how easily we begin comparing our children? How we begin using their accomplishments as a measuring stick for how we feel about ourselves? Hang around any playground, practice field, or graduation ceremony and you'll find parents brimming with pride, and quick to give their child a leg up in conversation by subtly putting someone else's down.

For the unofficial Stork Derby that went on in Jacob's home, the final count was thirteen in all, twelve boys and one girl, a baker's dozen of blessing. But no one seemed to be counting their blessings. They all seemed to be keeping score. The life-sized scoreboard for this giant competition was kept in the naming of the children.

Leah's children tell a particularly sad story of longing to be loved. Some of those were Reuben (God sees my misery), Simeon (God hears my cry), Levi (surely my husband will become attached to me now). Leah names one of her sons Zebulun, or "dwelling" (maybe my husband will dwell with me now that we have this many sons together). Rachel dubbed the children born to her maid to indicate the depth of struggle she experienced with her sister. They were Naphtali (with great wrestlings I have wrestled with my sister, and I have prevailed) and Dan (God has judged me the winner and given me a son). When Rachel finally experienced a long-awaited gift of a pregnancy of her own, she named the child Joseph, or "may God add"—as in "please add another son to my side of the scoreboard."

Even though her lifelong dream of giving birth to Jacob's son was fulfilled, she was not even able to rejoice in the blessing she had been given because it was never enough. She wanted more. She wanted to win.

The rivalry between these two sisters, married to the same man, was so intense that later when the laws of Leviticus were written, this one was included: "You must not marry your wife's sister as a rival and have sexual contact with her while her sister is alive" (Leviticus 18:18).

I'm sure the initial readers of that law would have murmured "Rachel and Leah" under their breaths as they nodded in agreement.

The question that begs to be answered after this lifetime filled with bitter competition is this: Who won? In the end, no one did. Rachel had Jacob's love but felt like a failure at giving him children. Leah's many sons were no consolation for her botched marriage.

They were both losers. Both lost the love and support and friendship of a sister who could've rejoiced at her baby showers, helped corral lots of little mischievous boys, shared secrets and recipes, and loved one another through a difficult life together. They lost the chance at sisterhood and closeness and support.

Their sons lost too. They grew up competing with each other because that's what their mothers taught them. They learned that family was more about who is winning than who is loving, more about one-upping others than supporting and encouraging them. As they became adults, their competition grew angry and violent, and they nearly brought the rivalry of their mothers to the level of a global disaster.

The final loss of their competition was the deepest blow, as the family lost Rachel herself. When God did "add" to her number a second son, she died giving him life, naming him with her last breath: "son of my sorrow." Jacob couldn't bear to give the boy such a sad label and renamed him Benjamin, "son of my right hand."

At the end of the lifelong match, guess who was left to care for all twelve of those little boys and one little girl, including the tiny baby Benjamin? Leah. I wonder how often she wished for her sister as she managed the next generation of sibling rivalry that ensued.

Comparison is toxic. It brings the sense that what I have, who I am, is never enough. It robs us of the ability to find joy in what we have while depriving us of the chance for relationship unencumbered by resentment. It often starts in families, but very rarely stays there. Often we carry on into our adult lives with the idea that others are the yardsticks that tell us if we measure up. The unspoken goal becomes anything with an *er* on the end: to be better or smarter or wealthier or healthier or happier than someone else.

A former professor of mine had been a missionary to Papua New Guinea in the years before modern convenience arrived in the remote villages. When he first moved there, he noticed many differences in the culture from that in the Western world—including that most people had a fairly healthy body image. There was no emphasis on dieting or exercise (what strange concepts in a world where people walk several miles a day by necessity and struggle to get enough food for their families to eat) and there were no words in their language for eating disorders such as anorexia or bulimia.

When electricity came to the isolated villages, he remembers long cords connecting mud huts, the blue lights of television shining through the spaces in the thatched walls. As TV moved from a new novelty to a nightly staple, a strange new phenomenon also spread. Girls and young women began to develop eating disorders. They had begun seeing a different standard for physical appearance than they were used to, piped in from the West, and they began going to physical extremes as they compared themselves with the new images of bodies they saw on television.

So here's a question: How would we even know if we were fat or thin unless we had someone to compare ourselves to? How would we know if we were rich or poor unless we were using what someone else had as a standard? Do you live in a big house? That depends on the house next door. Do you have a lot of money? It will depend on whether you're making side glances at the multimillions on Wall Street or the two dollars a day people live on in Bangladesh.

The problem with constantly comparing ourselves with others is that it's such an arbitrary measure of life. We either come out on top and feel superior and prideful, or we find ourselves sinking to the bottom of the heap.

Meanwhile, as we are busy comparison shopping ourselves to death, God has a much greater way of pricing our value. "You are not your own; you were bought at a price" (1 Corinthians 6:19-20 NIV).

We have already been bought and paid for, and the price paid for us was the life of the perfect Son of God. If we had been worth any less, do you think he would have paid the ultimate price? If God considers us to be worth this much, who are we to go around discounting ourselves? The price tag we wear does not say "Marked down" or "Damaged, sell as is" or "Great bargain." It says, "Created by God. Lost to sin. Bought back at a premium. Worth the greatest price ever paid."

God does not love us because we won any contest, or because we have the most of anything or are the best at anything. He loves us simply because we are his. It's not worth the consequences that comparing brings to try to measure up to anything else.

Valerie Monroe, beauty director at O, The Oprah Magazine, says she grew up comparing herself not to a sister but to her own mother. Her mom was a model, a beautiful woman that she describes as a "full-blown goddess."

She remembers standing and staring into the mirror when she was a small girl, looking at her mother and then at herself, the two of them dressed in matching outfits. Aside from their ensembles, they looked nothing alike. One she describes as a goddess. The other, "a skinny, freckle-faced tadpole." As she shifted her gaze from one to the other, looking up and down at herself and her mother, Valerie perfected the fine art of comparison. As she grew up, she continued to define herself by how she compared to other women. Although she outgrew the skinny tadpole stage, she never quite outgrew the practice of sizing herself up to the woman next to her. Today, she says, she is a mature fifty-one. But her stubborn comparing mind is still stuck at six years old. She describes a situation in which she tried to overcome the comparison rut when a gorgeous young woman crossed her path on a busy street:

> "Bad luck for you!" cries my comparing mind. "You'll never look like that again! You're old and invisible!"...Her beauty imbues her with a mild haughtiness. In a regal kind of way, she turns her head in my direction....
>
> "You," I say, "are simply magnificent."

The young woman's haughty air vanished. Caught off-guard, she was at first suspect. But sensing no ulterior motive, she flashed a wide, beautiful smile toward Valerie and thanked her for the compliment. Valerie responded,

> "It's my pleasure to tell you," I say, and it is. Because I not only remember how happy I have felt as the recipient of an authentic compliment, but now I have enjoyed the additional gratification of being able to give one.[2]

After years, Valerie still struggles to deliberately lay down her instinct to compare, to view others as rivals to her own status. But she consciously and repeatedly strikes down the voice that tells her that if beauty resides in another, it cannot also reside in her. She is finding a new role: "Appreciator of All Things Beautiful."

Can we celebrate beauty when it resides in someone else?

Can we announce the blessings that we see in the people around us, even if it means forgoing the chance to feel superior or envious?

We are surrounded by Leahs and Rachels, those who feel unwanted and unloved, underserved and underblessed. Could a simple blessing from our own lips fall on those who need words of assurance today? There is so much beauty to be acknowledged in the world. Who will call it out? Will I? Will you? These words of affirmation and encouragement could do so much, could cancel the competitions and begin instead a new season of friendship. It's time to drop the contest that never mattered anyway, and pick up instead the role of appreciator of all things beautiful, especially when beauty resides in the other, who may just need to hear us point it out.

CHAPTER 9

Joseph
Change

WHEN GOD WANTS TO CHANGE the world, he starts with a family. But what happens when he needs to change a family? What happens when the path of one clan of people is stuck driving in ruts that are well-worn but harmful?

Christmas dinner at my grandmother's house has always been prepared with love and holiday cheer, and a system of well-developed hierarchy that would rival any military operation. Each of the dishes on the menu carries a rank, defined by its degree of difficulty, and each of us—my mother, my aunt, and myself—is assigned a dish based on our position on the family totem pole.

Each year, the four of us gather in the kitchen, which has been the hub of our family for over forty years, and gravitate almost immediately to our stations, my mother by the stovetop for the hot dishes, my aunt near the pantry where she'll assemble the pies, while in the commanding officer position, my grandmother rotates among us, handing out recipe cards and giving instructions. I take my place at the cutting board by the sink to prepare the candied apples.

For as long as I can remember, the candied apples have been my job for the Christmas meal. I've leaned across the counter for years and watched the preparation of the turkey, dressing, and pies, until the time came for the apples. Every year since I was old enough to stand on a stepstool at the kitchen counter, I have carefully taken cherry-red slices of apples, cooked in sugar water and red food coloring, and arranged them in the shape of a poinsettia flower on a large serving plate. In the beginning, my job consisted of the arranging alone, but in recent years I had actually been trusted to peel, cut, and cook the apples. Always under a carefully watchful eye, of course, to make sure I got it right. I've eaten every Christmas dinner in memory with bright red fingertips.

This is the only time we cook together—my mom, aunt, grandmother, and me. It's the only time of year we do a lot of things. Like fancy placemats. And assigned seating at the dining room table. And feigning intimacy with more distant family members (who would come once the meal was prepared), as if we saw them every week and not twice a year, taking the same family picture in front of the same Christmas tree each year to create a carefully staged memory. And gravy. What other meal in the entire year requires a big boat full of gravy?

That was the question running through my mind one year as I looked at the recipe card in my hands, turning it over and looking at the splotches and stains, the yellowed edges and slanted script that runs in my family, making it impossible to tell if this card had been written by my mom, my grandmother, or perhaps by her mother at some point. As old as this card was, this was the first time I'd ever held it in my hands, the first time I'd ever seen it, actually. My grandmother had thrust the card into my hands as I stood unsuspectingly at my cutting board waiting for my apple assignment. No explanation, just, "You make the gravy." I was awed by the responsibility and significance of this sudden promotion.

I bristled a bit when I realized I would need my mother's help to figure out this recipe, ages old in the family but new to me that Christmas. Coming home from college for the holidays meant slipping into the groove of the family, into familiar roles that I wanted to be rid of but couldn't seem to avoid. Taking orders from her about cooking would mean that my mother knew better than I, that I was following in her footsteps. Mostly, I was unwilling to hear any message that came from my mother's lips that year. I was battling for identity in a way all twenty-something girls do, by defining myself as "not my mother." I would go through life making choices that were the opposite of the choices she had made; I would choose the other half of the fork in any road. I was careful to stay two or three steps from her as I crisscrossed the kitchen, gathering the ingredients on the card.

My experience in the kitchen was so limited that I stopped and stared at the recipe for gravy as if it were written in Chinese: "Place melted butter in a heavy saucepan and stir in the flour. Cook and stir for three to five minutes, or until butter barely begins to turn golden...." I'd melted the butter in a daze and had the cup of flour poised above the pan, ready to pour, when my mom cried out abruptly, "Not like that!" I froze. Just as suddenly, she turned away and began opening cupboards behind her. "You need a..." Her voice trailed off as she disappeared into the cabinet where she began searching for the thing I apparently "needed."

It was not an easy task finding something in these cabinets. My grandmother has her own version of recycling called, "Keep everything. You may need it someday." I had no idea what my mom was looking for, but I knew it was going to take her a while.

As she rummaged, my mother kept talking, her voice coming hollow and wooden from inside the ancient cabinets. "You know I almost failed home ec class, right? The first time I ever made gravy was in home ec in junior high. The teacher made this perfect little pot of it to demonstrate, and then we were all to go to our own little stations and follow her model exactly....Only when I stirred mine together, I did something wrong and the flour clumped up into these ugly lumps in the pan. And there was the teacher, walking from station to station, grading everyone's gravy, getting closer to mine, and I was about to fail." Her voice trailed off into a cupboard.

She had told me stories of this mysterious land called home ec before. Failing home ec was like failing being a woman. For girls in those days, home ec was a requirement, not an elective. It was your major from the day you got your first toy kitchen set. If you wanted a career, you had your choice of teacher, secretary, or nurse, but that was only until you found a husband and your true career started as homemaker. The world she was describing was like a fairy-tale land to me, something like the fate of Cinderella, unknowable except in stories.

"What happened when the teacher saw your lumps?" I asked, when she came up for air between cabinets.

"She never did. While she was walking around checking the other girls' pots, I took a spoon and ate the lumps. Every one of them. Gave me a stomachache, but I got an A!"

Inspired by the memory of her success, she reached into the cabinet above the stove and pulled out a glass jar with a metal lid. Pouring warm water and flour into the jar, she shook it until it was a creamy mixture and then handed it to me, gesturing for me to continue.

"Look," she said, "no lumps."

"Did you learn that in home ec?" I asked, gingerly taking the jar from her fingers, our wrists meeting briefly in the space between us.

"I guess I just figured it out through trial and error," she shrugged, turning back to whatever was on the stove before her: cranberry sauce? oyster stuffing? something more complicated than gravy.

For a moment, I just stood there staring at the jar in my hands, the butter and flour now mixed nicely into a beautifully smooth concoction. Somehow, the fact that the magic of forty years ago still worked meant that there was a chance that the recipe she had handed me for life might be viable after all. I looked up from the jar to my mother, stirring something at the stove. She was right about something. Maybe she was right about other things as well.

That image of my mother eating the lumps out of her gravy has stuck with me over the years. She took the lumps and then found a new way so that I didn't have to. This happens in so many families—the one person, the one generation, who takes the lumps, changes the patterns, finds a new path, so that the next generation doesn't have to experience the same pain and struggles.

When God wants to change a family, he starts with just one person. One person willing to change the patterns of the past by having wisdom and courage to steer in a new direction. The Genesis family was sorely in need of that one person. They were chosen by God, designated as his emissaries to receive his blessings and spread them out to the whole world. God had chosen their family to change the world.

But what if the family God chooses has more issues than National Geographic? What if they have trouble obeying? Countless preapproved choices in the garden and they still eat the one fruit called forbidden. What if they have trouble getting along? Brother turned against brother, sister competing with sister. What if they are called to be a blessing to the whole world, but they can't even find their way to kindness within their own household?

When the family God chooses is full of black sheep, betrayers, and scoundrels, how will God's plan succeed? When the odds are so stacked against him, how will God go about making a difference in that family so they can make a difference in the world?

When God wants to change a family, he starts with just one person.

And as usual, God chooses the underdog. Joseph.

He's penultimate in birth order, the second to last of Jacob's twelve sons. He has the vision for great leadership, but lacks the maturity to produce a following. Charisma, while it may draw people to leadership, can't gather a crowd without a healthy dose of humility behind. Joseph is a braggart and a brat. He goads his brothers with tales of his dreams and wears the mantle of hurtful favoritism: a special coat given to him by their father.

My father grew up in a family of four boys. There were a lot of homemade clothes and hand-me-downs for this family who lived simply in a dusty, West Texas town. There weren't many new clothes, and those were usually for special occasions. If your brother wore holes in the knees of a perfectly good pair of pants, your mother patched them and they became yours.

If hand-me-downs were the norm in a family of four boys, in this family of twelve brothers, what is the eleventh in line doing with a new coat? Here is an obvious signal that this is Jacob's favorite son, but it may have also indicated his choice of a successor, the one who would inherit the birthright and become patriarch after Jacob was gone.

In Jacob's family of origin, the favoritism their parents showed Jacob and Esau wreaked havoc on family relationships and drove the family apart. In Jacob's family of choice, his favoritism of his favorite wife Rachel over Leah drove a wedge between the sisters and forever marked their family. Now, after Rachel's death, Jacob begins to favor Joseph over all of his other sons—probably because Joseph reminded him so much of Rachel. If pitting one brother or sister against the other can cause tragic consequences, just imagine what it can do to a family when a father indulges one brother out of twelve.

The Genesis family seems to be in deeper trouble than ever before, and they're running out of time to fix things. This is the last generation on the record, so they have to get it right quickly.

The key to transforming the family, and their story, is the transformation of Joseph. As the old adage puts it, "Good judgment comes from experience. But experience comes from bad judgment."

Joseph is certainly the recipient of a lot of bad judgment: His own for sharing his dreams of grandeur with his brothers (whether he is the center of the universe with them orbiting him, or he is the tall sheaf of grain with theirs bowing to him, the message always seems to be the same.) His father's for not recognizing what his preferential treatment is doing to the family. And his brothers' most of all. When Joseph is sent into the fields where they are working to check up on them as their father's emissary, they seize him in anger with certain plans to kill him later.

In the midst of their murderous schemes, two brothers

step out in Joseph's defense. First, Reuben encourages the brothers not to kill him but to throw him in a pit and leave him there. Deciding to do just that, they seize Joseph, confiscate his coat, and roughly toss him into a dried-up cistern. Then they sit down to calmly discuss the matter over lunch. As they do, another brother, Judah, sees a band of traders passing by as an opportunity to suggest that they sell Joseph into slavery. Though harsh treatment, this may be what prevents Joseph's death.

Reuben's kindness, in particular, is striking. When he returns to the cistern to rescue Joseph—evidently having been absent when they sold Joseph into slavery—he weeps and tears his clothes as a sign of grief. Since Reuben is the eldest of all the brothers, he is the one who should be most threatened by Joseph's potential rise from the bottom of the heap to become the heir. It is Reuben's birthright that is at stake here if Joseph continues his rise in power within the family.

After the brothers slaughter a goat and cover Joseph's coat with its blood, they return together to their father, hand him the blood-stained coat, and say as little as possible about where it came from, letting Jacob draw his own conclusions. Refusing to be comforted, he pledges to mourn for his favorite son until he himself joins him in the grave.

What will become of our dreamer? Although the dreams God pledged for this family have never been on shakier ground, there is no doubt that God can turn even this situation around. Indeed, he loves to find the most hopeless of dreams and help them become a reality.

The trouble with dreams is that sometimes the dreamer isn't ready. In Joseph's case, the dreams are all true. But the dreamer needs work before the dream can be realized. If God had handed Joseph the power and position he desired at this early and immature stage of his life, Joseph probably would not have handled it well. Instead, Joseph will have to wait until he is ready, allowing his character and trust in God to develop through the years.

When God wants us to accomplish big things for his kingdom, he must first prepare in us big character to match big vision.

This whiplash from the sudden overthrow of his comfortable lifestyle is a good indication of the future Joseph is about to face, since the next few chapters find Joseph hanging on for the roller-coaster ride of his life. Just when life knocks him down, Joseph will suddenly rise up. Then just as he begins to get on his feet, he lands suddenly flat on his face again. *Suddenly* might be Joseph's middle name, since the word is implied around every corner of his story. His life changes as suddenly as the climate in my home state of Texas, where we like to say, "If you don't like the weather, just wait a minute!"

Slavery is not an enviable station in any culture, but Joseph somehow makes the best of it. He prospers as the second in command to his master Potiphar, and the leadership gifts that came across as pride in his youth now develop into full flower. Just as he is coming into true success, his master's wife propositions him, then turns the tables when she's scorned and falsely accuses Joseph of being a sexual predator.

First defrocked of his precious coat by his brothers, Joseph is now literally stripped of his dignity and reputation by his boss's wife and thrown into prison. Twice now Joseph has been victimized—once by his own family with violence, theft, and human trafficking; and now by his employer with sexual harassment, slander, and false imprisonment. What's noteworthy is that he never plays the victim. Joseph continues to show character and perseverance when most people might have given up. Unlike his father, Jacob, Joseph does not deceive others or manipulate situations for his own gain. Joseph is honest and hardworking and never lets a tough situation keep him down. His perseverance and God's presence means that he's able to bloom where he's planted, even in the darkest of dungeons.

While in prison, Joseph's inwardly focused gift for dreaming turns outward when he begins to interpret other people's dreams. Word gets back to the Pharaoh, who needs a good dream interpreter, and after fulfilling his promise to interpret the Pharaoh's dream, Joseph once again ends up the second in command, this time over all the kingdom.

Pharaoh's dream means that tough times are ahead for Egypt, and it might not have worked in Joseph's favor to be the bearer of this bad news. So, instead of simply dropping the news of a severe famine in Pharaoh's lap for him to deal with, Joseph also proposes a set of sensible solutions, suggesting that "Pharaoh look for a discerning and wise man and put him in charge of the land of Egypt" to prepare the country for the worst (Genesis 41:33 NIV). The power of suggestion works, Pharaoh recognizes the gifts of discernment and leadership in Joseph, and suddenly Joseph goes from convict to cabinet member.

First Potiphar, then the prison warden, and now Pharaoh recognize Joseph's remarkable gifts. Pharaoh is so impressed with Joseph that he elevates him to be his right-hand man. This time, Joseph is not running a household or a prison but an empire. Wherever Joseph goes, God blesses him; and when he is blessed, he doesn't hesitate to give credit to God. Our little braggart is growing up.

Joseph experiences God's goodness in the throne room and in the dungeon. God's blessings are not like a faucet that is turned on in good times and off in bad. God is constantly blessing us, whether our circumstances are favorable or not. God is with us in hard times, but even more than that, God is blessing us at all times. And we can learn to recognize those blessings, whether they come to us on a mountaintop of success or in the deep valley of struggle, by maintaining an attitude of thankfulness and gratitude.

Joseph is now beginning to see those earlier dreams of leadership and success come true—but not before watching the dreams go down the drain more than once. As we've noted previously, often when God gives us a dream, it takes time for it to unfold. Sometimes, like Joseph, we see our dreams go through distinct phases:

- the birth of the dream
- the death of the dream
- the rebirth or resurrection of the dream

The hope present throughout Joseph's story is not that God makes the lives of his children easy or carefree but that God is present in our cares and struggles. It is never easy to witness the death of a dream, but if we are faithful to see it through to the end, the dream often emerges with God's help in a way that is even better than before.

That happens so clearly here in the very last phase of the family story. Thanks to Joseph's foresight, when the famine hits at its hardest, Egypt has enough grain stored up to support not only its own people, but the surrounding nations. Families pour in with requests for food, selling off their own land to Egypt's growing empire in return for rescue.

One day in his throne room, Joseph's dreams begin shaping reality as a family of ten brothers (and one left behind and home) from a neighboring country walks in, desperate for help from the Egyptian empire. When the brothers arrive, they don't recognize the powerful man before whom they are forced to beg for grain. Joseph is older now, probably clean shaven and clothed in the costume and headdress of Egyptian rulers. But Joseph recognizes his brothers immediately. From our point of view as readers, we can see Joseph's emotions fluctuate.

While the brothers see only one side of the story, we can see a man who is struggling with confronting his past and what to do with the power he now wields over the brothers who wronged him. For a while he toys with them like a cat with vulnerable prey, first keeping one brother in prison in Egypt while sending the rest of them home to guarantee he will see them again. Then he sends them home with bags stuffed with grain and the insistence that they return with their younger brother Benjamin. On the way home they realize (with a sinking feeling) that the money they paid for the grain is still in their bags. Joseph repaid the grain fee secretly, but to the brothers it seems they accidentally shoplifted from a very powerful man.

When they must return for more grain (not out of a desire to rescue their imprisoned brother), they know that they have to bring Benjamin as part of the deal. The terrible burden this separation brings to their father reveals how protective the whole family is of Benjamin, the youngest and their father's surviving son from his favorite wife.

Upon seeing his younger brother again, Joseph alternates between moments of tenderness and the outward appearance of an angry tyrant. In an apparent act of revenge on the ten brothers, he falsely accuses Benjamin of stealing and insists that he will make Benjamin his slave and force the brothers to return home without him, an act that might kill their father with grief. The brothers who once carelessly tossed Joseph aside without a thought for their father's feelings are beside themselves with concern for Benjamin and for their father's heartache.

If we are able to read this story as if for the first time, not knowing what will happen on the last page, it would be very clear at this point that Joseph's desire for vengeance is winning over his tendency to show compassion or forgiveness. It appears that the one brother he cares for, Benjamin, will remain with him and the others will face an unknown fate.

Joseph's calculated acts of revenge are becoming clear:

- he wrongfully imprisons Simeon, just as he was wrongfully imprisoned by Potiphar;
- he falsely accuses the brothers of spying and stealing, just as he was falsely accused by Potiphar's wife;
- and now, in a last act of payback, Joseph is threatening to make Benjamin his slave, just as his brothers cruelly sold him into slavery, taking a favorite son from their father just as he was taken.

One by one, Joseph is reenacting the wrongs done to him in the cruelty he visits on his brothers. Those hearing Joseph's story for the first time have to wonder and worry: What will he do next? Are his brothers' lives in danger? His family history doesn't leave us much hope, since between Cain and Abel and, more recently, Jacob and Esau and Rachel and Leah, there is a long history of those within the same generation choosing self-interest over fraternity.

The game-changing moment comes when one brother steps forward from the pack. All of the brothers are panicking over the possible loss of Benjamin. All of them are anticipating the grief of returning home without him, having lost yet another brother, the youngest and now favorite son of their father. But Judah alone offers a solution. He volunteers to trade places with Benjamin, sacrificing his own life and his future so that Benjamin will have a future and their father will be spared the immense grief all the brothers are dreading. Judah alone knows the power of sacrifice. This single act melts Joseph's heart and allows healing to begin in the family.

Sacrifice moves people. Sacrifice jolts us out of our daily routine of putting "me first" and makes us wonder, *Why would you go out of your way for me? What could possibly motivate you to put my interests before your own?*

Judah's act of sacrifice changed the course for this family, just as the selfless acts of many people before him and since have shaped families to be places where we learn to care for others with generous hearts.

When God's plan to use this family to save the world finally plays out in the end, the central figure of this plan—a descendant of Adam and Eve, of Noah and his clan, Jacob and Esau, Rachel and Leah, Joseph and all the rest—will be Jesus himself. He will put on the flesh and blood and DNA of this family. Jacob's twelve sons will become the heads of twelve tribes, creating a new taxonomy for all who will be born into the family from now on.

When Jesus enters the family it won't be through the tribe of Reuben the firstborn, or through the two tribes who come from Joseph the hero's lineage. Jesus will be born into the tribe of Judah.

The family calling that God gave to Abraham and Sarah predicted that they would be "blessed to be a blessing" to all the nations. In one respect, Joseph's position in Egypt fulfills that prediction because Egypt and the surrounding nations are blessed by Joseph's foresight and leadership. But the larger blessing comes when God sends his own Son, Jesus, to be born into this family, and his sacrifice brings the greatest blessing the world has ever known. Jesus is born with a pedigree of sacrifice, the Lion of the Tribe of Judah. The lineage of sacrifice that turned the tide for Joseph's family would bring the ultimate sacrifice that would bring blessing to all people.

The moment Joseph hears Judah pledge to give his life and serve as a slave in exchange for their little brother's freedom, Joseph's cruel facade breaks down. He sends all the Egyptians out of the room, comes down from his place of authority to approach his brothers, and reveals his identity. They are immediately horrified and afraid for their lives, knowing the punishment they deserve and Joseph's power over them. But he reassures them that his attitude toward them is one of forgiveness.

While past generations of the family (Cain and Abel, Isaac and Ishmael, Rachel and Leah) showed no signs of reconciliation, Joseph finds the courage to pursue a path of peace for the future of this family. For generations, this family has lived with a script of competition and revenge. Their father Jacob and his brother, Esau, had an encounter of forgiveness, but we have no record of their relationship after that moment to know if the relationship was restored. Joseph chooses a new path, unlike his ancestors, to forgive his brothers and live in peace with them.

Joseph is the family member who breaks the family cycle and begins a new way of relating within the family. Whatever cycles have played out in your family in the past, you were not meant to stay in an ongoing cycle of defeat. God calls us to be new creations, to chart a new course as the first generation that chooses a new path.

When God wants to change the world, he starts with just one person. Every family needs one. Every family needs a Joseph. Someone who looks back at the past, puts their foot down, and declares that the future will be different—that they won't be defined by their family's past. Every family needs at least one individual, one generation, that makes a change that will make things different for every generation to come.

I know just how important this pivotal person can be because I have one. I have a Joseph. My Joseph is my mom.

I have some sympathy for the Genesis family, with all of their generational conflicts, dysfunctions, and quirks recorded in Scripture for all of posterity to read. If the world somehow discovered my family's history, they would find it has all the interesting earmarks of a soap opera—with conflict, addiction, abuse, divorce, and lots more.

Instead of continuing some of the destructive patterns of the past in our family, my mom made every effort to drive out of the ruts that had been well-worn for generations and make a new path for us. People always notice my mom's eyes when they meet her, wide and full of expression. They show just about every feeling she has. Poker is not a game she could win, even if she felt like trying. Old photo albums show a look of woundedness in her eyes in one season of life, but turning the pages you'll find determination in the next. It's the look of peace that I see in her on the later pages that amazes me. Some combination of stubbornness and surrender made her who she is today, eyes shining with love and generosity and self-acceptance.

Because of my mom's willingness to let Jesus reshape her and the family she would influence one day, my family history is just that: history. It's no longer our present reality. And it sure isn't our future.

Every family needs a Joseph, that one person that we can look back at and see that because of them, every generation afterwards has a chance at a new path, a new direction. When God wants to change a family, he uses the willingness of one person to change and uses them to make a difference for generations to come.

I wasn't aware of the way my mom had taken the lumps for me until years later. Childhood is an ignorant bliss of thinking your parents can do no wrong, then years of thinking they can do no right, then the realization that they are human and do both every day, just like everyone else. At age ten I slept through a hurricane, cozy upstairs in my bed, while she moved our prized possessions upstairs one by one as a few inches of water flooded into our first floor. She had been careful to step lightly on the stairs as not to wake me. What else had I slept through while she moved our lives in ways that would protect me? How many times had she eaten the lumps so that things would come out smooth in the end?

When Joseph finally revealed himself to his brothers, they cowered before him. The knowledge of the violence, the retribution between brothers in generations past was fresh on their minds and in their history. They were sure Joseph was about to lash out, so they bowed low before him, fulfilling his childhood dreams of sheaves of wheat. Instead of violence, they felt his hands on them with gentleness, lifting their faces from the ground. What he told them next was shocking.

"As for you, you meant evil against me; but God meant it for good" (Genesis 50:20 NKJV™).

Joseph can not only forgive but also see God at work even in the worst moments—one move ahead of evil on the chess board every time. Sometimes we say that "hindsight is 20/20"—but Joseph has more than that. He can see clearly not just that the hard times worked out OK in the end, but that God was blessing, moving, working behind the scenes in his family, even when things were toughest. Because of where that verse is found in Genesis, it's been called "50/20 vision": the ability to look back and see the strength in the struggle, to know that the lumps were there, that the pain was real, but that God was at work all along.

Let me be very clear about this: God is not the author of evil. It is not his desire for us. Our hurts do not come from his hand. God doesn't cause our hurts—but he doesn't waste them either. He can use them to transform and change us. God's will is such a force that it cannot be stopped by obstacles.

That's why in this family, this flawed, messed up, normally abnormal, broken and blessed family, when God promised he would use them to change the world, nothing in the world could stand in his way.

Every family needs that person. The one who is changed and then becomes the agent of change, spreading a new season through their generations and those to come. We may look back and recognize it in generations past—the person whose blessings are still flowing to the rest of us. Or we may, instead, see a deep need still for that one person to emerge, grab hold of Jesus, and let the peace and transformation he brings change our families forever.

Every family needs a Joseph. If your family has needs that God wants to meet, that Joseph could be you.

CHAPTER 10

Picture Imperfect: God's Family
Communion

FAMILY PICTURES HAVE ALWAYS fascinated me. The day the church directory came out was one of my favorite days as a child. After the Sunday morning service that day, the ushers would hand each family a slim yearbook-style, spiral-bound book, filled with pages of full-color family photos followed by plain white paper filled with our Xeroxed phone numbers and addresses. As kids, we would flip through the pages to check out our friends' family pictures, giggling at their stiff, awkward poses in front of washed-out blue backgrounds. For many this tradition provided not just a visual reference to who was part of our community, but the opportunity to have a formal family portrait taken every couple of years.

After church, I would clutch the new directory on the way home, then run into the house to the shelf where all the previous directories were lined up. Pulling them out, I'd open them and lay them out side to side in chronological order on the floor in the dining room. Lying on my stomach, I would glance from one to the next, comparing pictures from year to year, watching as new babies were added and children changed through the years, noticing the mom's hairstyles grow bigger and bigger with the Texas fashions of the 1980s and 90s.

Most of all, I loved studying families: how a son had his mother's chin or a daughter mirrored the way her dad held his head, how everyone had brown eyes in one family, but in another only one child had red hair like their mom. I was a little student of genetics long before my biology degree compelled me to learn about dominant and recessive traits and the scientist/monk Mendel's studies with beans. It wasn't just resemblance that fascinated me, but relationship. How a group of people could belong to one another. How they could end up, year after year, in the same grouping, same poses, their life together filled with ordinary practices and strange secrets that the rest of us as outsiders were not privy to.

On the page with the G's and H's, I found my own family picture: my mom and me. I had her wide blue eyes, her auburn hair. But my angular profile stood in contrast to hers, the shape of my nose a mystery unless you knew my dad, who was not in the picture. In the middle of an open page of families with moms and dads and multiple children, we were the only family of one parent and one child. I thought about that a lot, how the shape of my own family was a slender sapling, while other family trees branched out to take up the whole frame. I made no secret of wanting brothers and sisters, hatching a secret plot at twelve years old to insist that my mom adopt a baby girl that we would raise together. But in reality I enjoyed the focused attention I got in our family of two. All children think themselves the center of the universe for a while. Those who grow up an only child actually experience it.

Our little family was small, but in no way were we isolated. The other pages of that directory showed faces so familiar that Sundays felt like a weekly family reunion. The Masseys were on the front page of the directory with the staff, since they were in charge of our music ministry at church. Besides being my choir director on Wednesdays and the organist at church on Sundays, Tish Massey was my piano teacher. Every Tuesday afternoon for twelve years, I went to her house where she fed me a snack, asked me about my day, and sat me down at her baby grand piano where she taught me about eighth notes, staccatos, and life. The Lamberts' picture showed the beautiful brown faces of their two daughters, a deep contrast to their parents. Their daughter was my best friend, and she and her sister were adopted as infants from our denomination's mission home for young mothers in crisis. I went to their house almost every day after school while my mom was working, and each afternoon when she came to pick me up, we were invited to stay for supper. I ate almost as many meals at their table as I did at my own. The Richardsons lived across the street and were among the many families we called "back-door friends." When I crossed the street to their house, I went past the front door and straight through the back gate. It was just understood that we would never knock, but walk in the back door and shout out a "hello!" On more than one occasion I slipped in, grabbed a Coke from their fridge, sat down on the couch, and punched the "on" button on the remote before the sounds of the TV alerted them that I was there. It felt as much like my house as theirs.

I knew the rough edges of these families as well as their posed smiles in the directory that came out every few years. I was in their homes enough to know the tensions and disagreements they circled frequently. Since we were together so often, even the dysfunctions I knew in my friends' families seemed normal to me, things to be expected. After all, they knew the cracks in mine as well.

Family trees are a funny thing to cultivate. The New Testament book of Romans describes the ancient horticultural practice of grafting a branch into a new tree.

"If some of the branches have been broken off, and you, though a wild olive shoot, have been grafted in among the others and now share in the nourishing sap from the olive root" (Romans 11:17 NIV). After it's severed from its original tree, a branch can be inserted into a cut made in a new one and then carefully bound, giving it every chance to flourish as part of an entirely new organism.

The fact that my own broken family was pieced together into the body of Christ saved me in more ways than one. Our collective life together, lived out in living rooms and church pews alike, gave me the kind of foundation that helped me draw from many family trees as I figured out what I wanted life in my family of destination to look like. Some people get just close enough to the church to find it filled with hypocrites and sinners and leave as quickly as they came. Discovering the imperfections of those who became family to me didn't drive me away at all. It confirmed that these families were fragmented like my own, struggling with God's help to make a life together. That's what I saw when I read Genesis as well, the family that began it all not even close to ideal, but loved anyway, made whole as they clung to God and each other. The descriptions of families as horticultural experiments in transplanting one branch to another to make a whole is clear about where the strength of the tree comes from: "If the root is holy, so are the branches" (Romans 11:16 NIV).

Years after my own seedling experiences in the family that formed me, I struggled to build a family of my own. After a lengthy battle, our family sprouted with an amazing little boy. When I was pregnant again, this time with a little girl, I remember talking to my mom, dreaming out loud of what our family would look like as they grew. I think I had that church directory picture in my head as a template of sorts, picturing us on the page, a family of four—a girl and a boy on mom's and dad's knees—everything I had dreamed of when I was a little girl staring at the complete families on the pages before me. Thinking out loud with that scene in my head, I said something like, "It's what I've always wanted. The perfect family."

"Don't do that." She said in a tone sharp enough to get my attention. "Don't do that to yourself. There is no way to have a perfect family." Then she reminded me of what I already knew, both from experience and the relationships with others she had done such a wonderful job building around us, that even the families that look perfect in the pictures struggle with something. That no family feels perfect all the time, that to set yourself up with only one picture in your head as the goal to be attained meant sure failure, but to love and accept the lot you've been given is to find happiness, contentment, success amid the imperfections. With God at the root, you're sure to find something better than sterile perfection. Something real. Something blossoming with joy.

It's not an either-or, broken or blessed. Every family knows both. Every family has seasons of struggle. And every family has moments that bloom with the inexplicable joy that comes from knowing you belong to someone, perfect or not. The God that blessed family from the very beginning knows all this, and he still invests in families, still uses them as the cradle and crucible in which our lives are formed and changed.

His family is big enough to hold us all in one frame, the picture packed with crazy uncles, black sheep, curmudgeonly grandparents, and mischievous newcomers. This is the family we belong to. Because we belong to him, we also belong to each other. The cuts in our family tree offer a tender opportunity for grafting, for a delicate shoot to enter and heal and thrive in a place where our sap runs clean with grace. This tree is a place where none of us is perfect, but together we are enough. And the enough comes not from our own strength, but from his embrace stretching out across us all. We are broken, and we are blessed.

BECOMING, BELONGING, BLESSING

This book invites you to become a student of families, including your own, those you interact with in everyday life, and the ones you interact with by reading about them in Scripture.

Instead of being a bystander, these interactions invite us to:

BECOME a better version of ourselves, one with even more family resemblance to Jesus.

BELONG to one another in meaningful ways, including adopting others into our Family of Choice

BLESS those whom God has placed in our lives and in our families.

It's my hope that reading *Broken & Blessed* will help you change and grow and that these exercises and questions will bring you into a more personal interaction with the words on these pages and move you (and your family) to an even greater place of blessing.

Becoming

Use these questions and exercises to help you think about becoming the son, daughter, parent, sister, brother, grandparent, friend whom God is calling you to be. Because families are dynamic systems, your pull in a God-ward direction will help your family stretch and grow as well.

Becoming a Student of Families

Today, say to at least two people: "Tell me about your family." Listen well. Then, if given a chance, tell them something about yours. Remember that transparency and openness with our own stories helps others feel as though they are not alone. Make sure to pray for those two people and their families before you sleep tonight.

Becoming a Student of Your Own Family

Do some research into your family of origin this week. Call or write an older relative and ask him or her to tell you a story about the family. Or look through some old pictures or letters and take a moment to remember those stories yourself. Where do you see God at work in your family's past?

Becoming an Instrument of Healing for Others

Sometimes the greatest thing we can do for those who have been hurt is to listen to their story. When someone begins telling you a story, put aside your desire to respond with your own story and simply listen, asking questions to clarify. If you know someone who is sick or struggling or has been hurt emotionally, call this person today and say, "What you're going through must be hard. What is that like right now?"

Belonging

Use these questions and exercises to become more connected to your own family, memories, loved ones, and to the One to whom you ultimately belong: God.

A Map of Belonging

Use the next page to draw a "life map" illustrating the points of milestones or highs and lows in your life or your family's life. It could be a drawing of a chronological time line or just a listing of major events. Take a step back and ask God to give you new insight into his presence in all of those stages. Share the life map with a friend or family member.

A Map of Belonging

A Tree of Belonging

Draw a family tree, going as far back as you can from immediate memory. Using memories or stories you've heard, write a description next to people who have brought blessings that have trickled down through the generations. Next to your own name, write some words describing the blessings you believe you bring to your family.

Belonging to Our Friends

In addition to those related to us by blood, we all have nonrelated people with whom we choose to journey through life. These are our Family of Choice. Make a list below of those friends who form your Family of Choice. Next to these names, write ways that you can support and encourage them today.

Belonging to God

Who are you prone to worry about, hold too tightly, or try to control, playing god in their lives? Write a prayer entrusting this person into God's hands and giving thanks that God loves him or her far more than you can image. If you pray more in pictures than words, draw a picture of the person in Gods' hands. Trust the Giver with the life of the gift.

Blessing

Use these questions and exercises to begin thinking of yourself as an agent of blessing, pouring out God's kindness into the world beginning with those closest to you.

Blessing the Next Generation

Write a letter to a young person in your family or your family of choice. This could be your son or daughter, grandchild, relative, neighbor, or the child of a friend. In the letter, tell this young person some hopes and dreams you have for his or her future. Include thoughts about how faith in God can make a difference in his or her life as well as advice about significant topics such as choosing a spouse or career. Let the young person know that you pray for him or her in these areas. Either send the letter to the person or keep it somewhere as a reminder to pray.

Blessing the Broken

Think of at least three individuals, families, or areas in the world that need reconciliation and healing. They may be conflicts between countries, people groups, political parties, family members, or friends. List their names and write next to each one the word *broken*. In a time of prayer, offer them each to God, cross out the word *broken*, and next to it write the word *blessed*.

Blessings of Forgiveness and Reconciliation

Are there families, perhaps even your own, that you know are in need of reconciliation? Pray for the return and reunion of family members separated by distance, whether emotional or physical.

Are there family members, possibly even yours, who struggle with resentment because of the actions of others in the family? Pray for the softening of hearts, for forgiveness, and for faces that shine with the love of Christ.

The Blessing of Family of Faith

Take a moment to think about being included in God's family. This means that you are related by faith to the people in Genesis and in Scripture who had faith in God. It also means that Christians around the world are part of your family. Make a list below of ways families care for one another. Beside this list, describe how you can support your family of faith locally and globally in similar ways.

Blessing with Our Actions

Think of someone who has had a difficult start in life because of the situation or choices of his or her family. It may or may not be someone you know personally. You also might think of a general part of your community (foster children, at-risk students, adults struggling with addiction, and so on). This week find a way to openly bless a person or group of people who need to feel blessings overflowing from the family of God.

Blessing with Our Words

Write a blessing for someone you love. Try to include some of the following elements: the power of positive words, the gift of unconditional love, some dreams or prayers you have for an outstanding future. When you are finished, send it in writing or read it verbally to the one you long to bless.

NOTES

3. A Family Manifesto // Chosen

1. "History Timeline," www.post-it.com/wps/portal/3M/en_US/PostItNA/Home/Support/About/.

2. The general concept for this section is from John Ortberg, "Would You Like Another Family?" (sermon, Menlo Park Presbyterian Church, Menlo Park, CA, January 12, 2008). www.mppc.org/sites/default/files/transcripts/080113_jortberg.pdf.

6. Rebekah // Cascade

1. John Ortberg, *The Life You've Always Wanted* (Grand Rapids: Zondervan, 2002), 82.

2. John Trent and Gary Smalley, *The Blessing* (Nashville: Thomas Nelson, 1993), 151–52.

7. Jacob and Esau // Competition

1. "Heartbreaking moment father dying of cancer walks his two daughters down the aisle because he knows he won't get to do it on their wedding day," *MailOnline*, September 13, 2013, www.dailymail.co.uk/news/article-2420613/.

8. Rachel and Leah // Comparison

1. Leon Kass, *The Beginning of Wisdom* (Chicago: University of Chicago Press, 2003), 423.

2. Valerie Monroe, "Life Isn't a Beauty Contest: How to Stop Comparing Yourself to Other Women," *O, The Oprah Magazine*, August 2002, www.oprah.com/spirit/How-to-Stop-Comparing-Yourself-to-Other -Women.